KIRKLEES HISTORICAL REPRINTS
VOL 2

HISTORY OF THE HUDDERSFIELD WOOLLEN INDUSTRY

By

W. B. CRUMP & GERTRUDE GHORBAL

KIRKLEES LEISURE SERVICES
THIS BOOK IS NUMBER

229

OF A LIMITED EDITION OF
1,000 COPIES

Kirklees Historical Reprints

Kirklees Libraries, Museums and Arts are proud to issue this series of
reprints of books of local historical importance. Each title will be
issued in a numbered limited edition that will not be reprinted in the
near future. The titles chosen will be of interest to local historians,
students and members of the general public who have an interest in the
social, economic and historical development of this part of the West
Riding of Yorkshire.

1. Frank Peel Spen Valley: Past and Present

2. W. G. Crump & G. Ghorbal History of the Huddersfield Woollen Industry

3. W. G. Crump Huddersfield Highways Down the Ages

ISBN 0900746 26 2

Quarter Leather 0 900746 34 3

These reprints have been specially produced and bound by Cedric Chivers Limited
of Bath for Kirklees Libraries, Museums and Arts

© 1988 Kirklees Leisure Services
Kirklees Libraries Museums and Arts H.Q.
Red Doles Lane
Huddersfield
HD2 1YF

Printed in Great Britain by
Dotesios Printers Ltd., Bradford-on-Avon, Wiltshire

COUNTY BOROUGH OF HUDDERSFIELD

THE

TOLSON MEMORIAL MUSEUM

PUBLICATIONS
EDITED BY
T. W. WOODHEAD, Ph.D., M.Sc., F.L.S.

HANDBOOK IX

HISTORY OF THE HUDDERSFIELD WOOLLEN INDUSTRY

BY

W. B. CRUMP, M.A.

AND

GERTRUDE GHORBAL, M.A.

HUDDERSFIELD:
PRINTED BY ALFRED JUBB & SON, LTD., ST. JOHN'S ROAD,
1935

There is no hiatus in economic development, but always a constant tide of progress and change in which the old is blended almost imperceptibly with the new.—E. LIPSON, 1931.

Surveying the old mines of the monks, the mills deserted a century or long years ago, and the admirable modern factories, you seem to see the process of industrial development (in the West Riding) like a slow-motioned film.—WILHELM TIETGENS (Berlin), 1932.

But the towns of the Pennines, old and new alike, are, or should be built of stone. . . . Even accumulated layers of smoke cannot overlay this fundamental unity of the Pennine towns with the country from which they spring. Unity is the exact word. . . . The Pennine towns are not *at one* with their surrounding country, they are one with it. And because the Pennine country is stark and resistant, the Pennine towns are stark and resistant. Nature not man made them so. These characteristics are implicit in the medium of which they are built.—KATHARINE C. CHORLEY, 1928.

Huddersfield—the district which produced, among other things, the dashing Victorian waistcoats of John Leach's pictures, and which, with the Tweed towns, was the pioneer of all modern fancy fabrics for men's wear, as opposed to the old broadcloths, friezes and pilot-cloths.—J. H. CLAPHAM, 1932.

3

CONTENTS

1. HOYLEHOUSE—A COLNE VALLEY HAMLET.

Florence E. Lockwood.

Photographed from a picture by Frances Lockwood.

5

ILLUSTRATIONS

PREFACE

More than ten years ago Miss Gertrude Humberstone, then newly graduated at Leeds University, made a rapid but intensive survey under my guidance of the woollen industry of the Huddersfield district in preparation of a thesis, and for this, when presented in 1925, she was awarded the first M.A. degree in Geography granted by the University of Leeds. Her subject was " The Woollen Industry of the Huddersfield District and its Relation to Local Geography, 1750–1925," so that after a brief sketch of the earlier domestic industry, Miss Humberstone's survey was concerned with the evolution and distribution of the industry under the influence of the new inventions of machinery and power. She based her primary survey on the sheets of the six-inch Ordnance Survey of 1851, dotted with "Woollen Mills," and on the maps of the Geological Survey ; and by making journeys through the district, by visiting textile mills of all types and by making enquiries from the older firms she gathered a large body of facts and expressed some of them in a map of " Industrial Distributions in the Huddersfield District," to be found in Chapter XII. The other group of facts relating to the history of individual firms and the success or decay of the " woollen mills " of 1851, she used extensively in her survey of the various river basins comprising the district.

These facts of distribution Miss Humberstone then correlated with the geographical and geological factors—the character of the rocks, the presence or absence of coal (and iron), the water supply both natural and artificial, and the improvement in means of communication and transport (roads, canals, railways). Her analysis did much to explain the historic development of the Huddersfield industry and in particular emphasised the horizontal division characteristic of the district, namely (1) the weaving or manufacturing centred in the old upland villages and hamlets, (2) the growth of new villages in the valleys, primarily engaged in spinning because they grew around the early water-driven scribbling mills. Nor did the contrast end there, for the late survival of hand-loom weaving on the hills and the slow conversion of the manufacturer's warehouse into a mill emphasised the difference as it does no longer. As pointed out by Mr. Fred Lawton, of Skelmanthorpe, " there were 170 handlooms in the cottages in Skelmanthorpe in 1890, and of these about a dozen were weaving fancy waistcoatings, twenty, Welsh shirtings, and the remainder were weaving plush goods."

I hoped that Miss Humberstone would be able to adapt her thesis to suit the general purpose of these Museum Handbooks ; but her marriage to Mr. Ghorbal and her removal to Egypt prevented her from carrying her study any further. She readily approved of my suggestion to place her material at the disposal of Mr. W. B. Crump, who proposed to broaden it into a history of the industry. He completed the first draft of this when the work was interrupted for the production of " The Leeds Woollen Industry, 1780–1820," published by the Thoresby Society in 1931. This in turn enabled Mr. Crump to deal more fully with the Huddersfield industry, and though there has been much unavoidable delay in the production of this handbook it has helped to widen and deepen the investigation. Miss Humberstone's work is the foundation of Chapters VIII. and IX. in particular, and the geographical aspect of her study is apparent in the " physical setting " of Chapter II. But it has been impossible to use all the historical details she gathered about individual firms and mills, though the examples quoted nearly all come from her collection. A copy of her thesis is preserved for reference at the Museum, so that the valuable facts she obtained by personal enquiry may not be lost.

Like previous handbooks this one has been written to promote the aims and to widen the influence of the Tolson Memorial Museum. It is complementary to the exhibits of textiles and textile machinery in the Museum. These tell the history of the woollen industry in one way, the handbook in another ; neither is complete without the other. Nor is either concerned with the equipment or organisation of the industry as it exists to-day. The handbook does not describe the exhibits, for the reader is invited to see them for himself. But the narrative does not overlook the homely implements of the domestic industry and the machines that displaced them ; the familiar interior of Wood's cropping shop is described with particular care as well as the shearing-frame, so famous by name through its tragic associations, and yet so unfamiliar in fact because not one appears to have survived.

Thanks are due to many manufacturers, more perhaps than can be named now, for their kindly reception of Miss Humberstone and the information they gave her. Amongst them were the late Sir James Hinchliffe, Messrs. G. Wrigley, of Cocking Steps, T. Woodhead of Meltham, the late Wm. Crowther of Slaithwaite, C. W. Beardsall of Huddersfield, T. Norton of Scissett, and H. Tomasson of Thurlstone. Sir Percy Jackson, of Messrs. Field & Bottrill, Skelmanthorpe, and Major Thomas Brooke, of Messrs. John Brooke & Sons, Armitage Bridge, both descendants of a long line of " clothiers " have placed both authors in their debt by supplying family history and giving access to business records. Mr. E. E. Eagland, agent of the Earl of Dartmouth, by allowing the Kaye and Dartmouth documents at Slaithwaite to be used, has also materially added to the value of the *History*.

Much thought has been given to the selection of the illustrations. Photographs have been specially taken by the late W. H. Sikes, and Mr. Stanley Shaw and Dr. J. Grainger have assisted not only with photographs, but also with copies of sketches, paintings, engravings and lithographs in the Museum to show the " habitations " of the industry, past and present. Thanks are also due to Mrs. Florence E. Lockwood for permitting the use of illustrations of the Colne Valley from her book *An Ordinary Life ;* Mr. Ammon Wrigley for the block of fig. 18 from his *Songs of a Moorland Parish ;* the Halifax Antiquarian Society for the block of fig. 8 ; Messrs. B. Brown & Sons for permission to reproduce the illustration of Wood's " Cropping Shop," fig. 19 ; Mr. H. R. Taylor, Estate Manager, for the plan of the Cloth Hall. Mr. J. F. Todd has drawn some of the maps, and Mr. D. Booth the line drawing of the Cloth Hall and Market Street from an oil painting in the Museum that could not otherwise have been reproduced. T. W. W.

CHAPTER I.

THE BEGINNINGS OF THE PENNINE WOOLLEN INDUSTRY.

The woollen industry of the Huddersfield district is a part of a greater textile industry that has existed since the Middle Ages on the flanks of the southern Pennines both in Lancashire and the West Riding of Yorkshire. The clack of the loom has been heard on the hills from the days when it was fed by the wool of the native moorland sheep, and a waterwheel lifted the stocks of a little mill on a moorland stream to full the cloth. Streams and moors and mills are at the very heart of the industry, and the loom has never deserted the hills though wool and cotton to feed it now come from the uttermost parts of the earth.

The beginnings of the Pennine industry are obscure in more than one sense. It arose in the humblest way as a domestic occupation to supply the needs of the family or of the hamlet, and then slowly discovered a wider market through local fairs. Because of its obscurity and insignificance this rural industry escaped recognition and regulation at a time when an organised cloth manufacture, sanctioned by the King and contributing to the revenue of the State, was flourishing in many cities and ancient boroughs of England under the control of craft gilds. The oft-repeated assertion that the cloth manufacture of the West Riding originated with the settlement of Flemish weavers invited to this country by Edward III. has no foundation in fact. There were fulling mills on the Aire and the Calder, and at Burnley, Colne and Manchester before he came to the throne. Skilled weavers would be, and were in fact, attracted to recognised centres such as York, where a good many Flemings settled after 1350. But in 1379 there were only seven, all of them from Brabant, scattered in the Riding at such places as Ripon, Skipton, Spofforth and Wetherby. The rough kersey cloth of the hills woven from the coarse wool of the moor sheep was beneath the notice of skilled workers from Bruges or Ypres. Though the Fleming is out of the question, there is strong reason for thinking that the Cistercian abbeys planted in the wastes at Fountains, Whalley and Kirkstall, Bolton Priory in Craven and more distant abbeys holding lands in the Pennines, all played a part in fostering the native industry. They were the great flock masters of the 13th and 14th centuries, and though most of their wool was sold to foreign merchants and exported through York and Hull in the 13th century, it is probable that by the 15th century much of the monastic wool was consumed at home.

But in these earlier centuries the Pennine industry was of no account in comparison with the output and reputation of the finer cloths produced at York and other corporate towns, such as Beverley, Hull, Ripon and Pontefract, where craft gilds and merchant gilds controlled the trade. The weavers' gild at York received its charter in 1164, and for three centuries York maintained its position at the head of the industry of the county, though there were many signs of decline towards the end. Medieval York was in fact a manufacturing and trading city of the first rank. The variety of its craft gilds is attested by the collection of *York Mystery Plays*, performed by them on Corpus

Christi day, one by each trade or mystery. In the cloth trade there were gilds of woollen weavers and coverlet (worsted) weavers, fullers and dyers, wool chapmen and wool packers, shearmen and woadmen. Iron workers included founders and smiths, armourers and makers of spurs and bits. Linking the two industries together were the wire-drawers and cardmakers, producing between them the hand-cards required by the woollen workers.

There were no corporate towns in the Pennines and only Wakefield shows any traces of town organisation. The collection of mystery plays known as the *Towneley Plays*, because the MS. long rested at Towneley Hall near Burnley, can now be definitely assigned to Wakefield, and is good evidence that craft gilds, which performed the plays, existed there in the 15th century if not earlier. The manuscript does not, as at York, give the name of the gild performing each play, but one is definitely labelled the " Litsters' (Dyers') Pageant " ; and in 1556 the Wakefield Burgess Court ordered that " everye crafte and occupacion doe bringe furthe (forth) theire pagyaunts of Corpus Christi daye as hathe bene heretofore used." This is the one link between the more ancient craft of the plain and the rural industry of the hills. Wakefield standing at the meeting of plain and hills passed on the older craft to the hills at its back and became the starting point of the Pennine industry.

The long drawn-out decay of the manufacture in York and its contemporary growth in the Pennines have been described by Professor Heaton in detail.[1] As a report in the Corporation Minute Books in 1561 put it, the reason why cloth making had passed from York to the " townes of Halyfax, Leedes and Wakefield " was that " the comodytie of the watermylnes is ther nigh at hande," besides cheap labour for the carding and spinning of wool. Tudor York found compensation for its vanishing craft in the prosperity of its Merchant Adventurers, who found profit in exporting the cloths woven in the Pennines, " kersies, bayes, cottons, northern dozens and other coarse cloths " to the annual value, it was claimed, of a million sterling. This was in 1601, and the list brief as it is, presents the Pennine woollen industry as a whole, for it includes Manchester " cottons," which were frized woollens, Rochdale bays, which were half worsteds, the narrow kerseys of Halifax and Huddersfield and the broadcloths of Leeds and Wakefield.

Three centuries of progress have since brought many changes ; cotton has all but ousted wool from Lancashire and has invaded the Yorkshire valleys ; worsted has shared the territory of woollens, and newer fibres and fabrics have challenged the older staples. Coal and iron have contributed to the evolution of the industry and have proved invaluable allies, furnishing it with power and machinery and enabling it to multiply a hundredfold, but they have set fixed bounds to its domain. And underneath all lies the human factor ; the inherited skill of the weaver, the courage, pertinacity and resourcefulness of the manufacturer. The industry has never failed to throw up

[1] *The Yorkshire Woollen and Worsted Industries*, Oxford, 1920, Ch. II.

men ready to face difficulties and surmount obstacles, whether mechanical or economic.

The following sketch of the woollen industry in the Huddersfield district attempts to trace its evolution from century to century, to gather the threads of the story and weave them into some orderly design. This is possible because the region is a natural one, with only one focus or market town. Nor has there been any break with tradition. Its historic woollen industry is still its principal industry ; even worsted came in too late to call for detailed presentation. There has been no influx of a foreign element, and the trade has essentially been an hereditary one, handed on from father to son for centuries much in the way that Miss Phyllis Bentley has described it for one century, with true insight, in her novel *Inheritance*.

There is another intimate picture of the manufacturer of this century to be found in a recent autobiography. In her unassuming narrative of *An Ordinary Life*, 1861–1924, Mrs. Florence E. Lockwood describes the new world she plunged into when she married Josiah Lockwood, of Black Rock Mills, Linthwaite. New to her and changing while she writes, and yet how old and how typical of the Colne Valley! Coming from the South and with the training of an artist, she found delight and happiness in the surroundings of a woollen mill. Her home was in the mill-yard—the house in which Josiah and his brothers had been reared and whose top storey had been added to hold the hand-looms. From this " embryo-mill " sprang the mill proper where the first small steam engine began to run in 1874. Her neighbours in the narrow lane up the Clough all worked at the mill, and she watched them as they passed her house.

" In these cottages live Nathan and Susanna, Sam and Ann, Peter the engine tender, Tom the huntsman, Bill the dyer, and others, all workers at the mill. . . . Old Sam Hayes, who " scarce ever " leaves the Clough, even at feast time, is tall and wiry and bearded, he is one of the oldest workers and has walked by like that on his way to t' mill since the day when the present masters were lads. The tall man who walks with him is his son and the little woman is Anna, his daughter. . . . Edward, the man in leggings wearing his hat jauntily, is one of the teamers. . . . Josiah's three brothers pass by, each with his own particular gait. Masters and men have grown up from boyhood to manhood in this quaint corner of the world, and they know each other."

" If I go out the housewives will look up and greet me as I pass by. On Thursdays the enticing smell of the week's " bake " greets me ; on Fridays, fettling day, I run the risk of a cold douche, for they syringe their windows with a vengeance and scrub their doorsteps and decorate them with a white edge lino. On Mondays the families' washed clothes festoon the route."

It is a homely picture that Mrs. Lockwood sketches, and Josiah in his home is drawn to perfection. Such as he are the men who have made the woollen industry of Huddersfield.

CHAPTER II.

THE PHYSICAL SETTING : MILLSTONE GRITS AND COAL MEASURES.

The industrial development of the southern Pennines is the outcome of the physical conditions or environment. Climate, elevation and configuration ; soil, rocks and minerals ; water supply and streams have all combined to provide a stage that has proved itself to be well adapted to the manufacture of cloth. Yet it was rather the natural disadvantages of the region, the rigorous and rainy climate, the barren shallow soil, the great moors and wastes, that first compelled a scanty population to turn to the raising of cattle and sheep and to the weaving of the home-grown wool. The Pennines were particularly stubborn ground for cultivation, as the summits were, except on the limestone, widely covered with deep peat, and the slopes often blanketed with boulder clay. The feudal lords used these moorland wastes as deer forests and raised cattle in vaccaries or booths on the upland pastures, making provision of hay for their winter keep ; on occasion they also mined lead and iron and smelted them with the brushwood of the forests. When they gave the monks places in these wastes whereon to live and labour they reserved rights of the chase to themselves, but the abbeys received rights of pasturage and of searching for minerals and of erecting forges in the woods. Their great flocks of sheep brought them wealth and the monastic working of iron in the heart of what became the textile area must also be ranked as scarcely less important in the industrial development of the region.

The wool-textile region may be defined as the hill country between the Craven Gap or Skipton in the north and the Derbyshire border, or Penistone and Ashton-under-Lyne, in the south ; and from Pendle Forest or Haslingden on the west to Wakefield and Leeds on the east. Those are not its present limits ; they are chosen rather to show the region as it was about the middle of the 18th century, since which it has receded before the invasion of cotton and iron. But as the modern industry still lies within the historic region that was its birth-place, there is the more reason for seeking in the physical conditions and natural resources of this region the causes of its stability and growth.

So the problem concerns the southern Pennines as a whole, and the characteristics of this region that distinguish it from the rest of the Pennine chain appear to be these :—

1. The plateau (regarded as the area above the 1,000 ft. contour) is neither as broad nor as high as in the mid-Pennines northwards, or the Peak of Derbyshire southwards. It is less massive and much more dissected by river valleys. The inclusion of the spur thrust out into Lancashire, between the Ribble and the Mersey, in no way detracts from this feature, though it adds to the breadth of the region.

2. The head waters of many rivers rise on the moorland summits and trench them with deep and narrow valleys (called cloughs in

their extreme form) that even in their lower courses were too steep-sided and too full of forest to admit of early settlement within them, or of roads along them.

3. A relatively large proportion of the whole region lies between 500 ft. and 1,000 ft. and this middle zone, lying between the valley edge and the moor edge, was the favoured site of early settlement. The places named in Domesday Book are nearly all upon it, as are most of the old villages, hamlets and farmsteads. For convenience, streams served as township boundaries, but the " town " was away from the stream and often much above it.

4. The core of the whole region is built of the Millstone Grits with a marginal fringe of Lower Coal Measures. The actual distribution is not so simple as that, and the fringe ends with a ragged edge in Airedale; but in effect the high moorlands and the valleys dissecting them are Grit country and the lower summits and slopes are on the Coal Measures. In Yorkshire the fringe is on the eastern margin ; in Lancashire there is a narrow fringe, but also a more important ring round the grits of Rossendale.

5. There is no limestone within the region, and consequently the water is everywhere soft and suitable for textile purposes. The industry shuns the limestone country both because of its hard water and of the comparative lack of springs and brooks on its fells and in its gills.

The well-watered but otherwise barren and inhospitable country of the Grits proved itself fitted to nurture the weaving of wool ; only it needed to be in contact with the Coal Measures to create a woollen industry. No conclusion emerges from the history of the industry more clearly than that its distribution has been dependent upon the contiguity of the Lower Coal Measures and the Millstone Grits. Both had abundance of soft water and of forest ; but the Coal Measures possessed greater wealth of ironstone and coal, their elevation was less, their soil deeper and habitable sites less bleak. So natural advantages weighted the scales in favour of the villages set on or near the fringe of the Lower Coal Measures. They became possessed of churches and their parishes ran far up into the hills, annexing all the Grit country with its smaller villages and townships. They became market towns and grew to be " clothing " towns—the centres of the cloth trade of their own wide parishes. With slight individual variations Huddersfield, Halifax, Bradford and Leeds on the one side, Rochdale, Bury, Burnley and Colne on the other have all risen in this way, risen in spite of the palpable disadvantages of some of their sites. Set among the hills they have had to struggle for centuries to improve their means of communication and transport.

The Grit country shared with the Lower Coal Measures the gift of abundant water supply, not only as streams but as springs on the hill sides. The latter comes about because the beds of porous sand-stones and gritrock are separated by impervious shales, which throw out the water on the hillside, or enable it to be reached easily by sinking a well. The alternation also produces a definite terracing o

2. Coal Measure 'Steps' Landscape, Almondbury.

a scarped hill side, as a comparatively level shelf of hard rock is succeeded by a steeper slope of more friable shale, until the summit is reached when again a massive rock like the Rough Rock or the Elland Flagstone forms an extensive level surface of gentle slope (Fig. 2). This geological structure has controlled the whole course of the economic development of the region. The towns and villages are not only built of the Rough Rock and the Elland Flagstone, and the farms on the hills of the Kinderscout Grit ; they are built upon these rocks where they outcrop on the slopes and summits. Hence many of the older villages have the appearance of being " hill-top towns," set on a spur or ridge high above the valley bottom.

Considering the Grit country more particularly, these upland villages had the moors at their back and the wooded river valley at their feet. Tillage under the harsh conditions imposed by their situation could only afford a meagre subsistence even though moorland and woodland furnished fuel for the home and grazing for some livestock. The common field system, the typical basis of the lowland village, was never more than a pale shadow of itself amongst the hills and crumbled to pieces at an early date. In the more remote townships there was not even a " town " nucleus, but only a number of scattered hamlets, none bearing the name of the township. Everywhere there was a super-abundance of moorland waste, and by the end of the 13th century piece-meal enclosures of the waste being encouraged within the great manor of Wakefield, which extended up Calderdale to the Lancashire border. In other districts the start might be later, as in Rossendale, where enclosure of the Forest only began early in the 16th century ; but once started, enclosure and improvement of small parcels of waste went on continuously until a township was largely parcelled out amongst a body of small-holders or yeomen, settled upon their individual holdings. There is no missing or mistaking these enclosures, for they are distinguished by the sturdy mullion-windowed farmsteads erected upon them, or refaced in stone, in the 17th century. They fringe the edge of the moor at 700 to 1,000 ft., or follow the contours of the valleys so far that the farms are now derelict and the patches of pasture and meadow gone back to moorland.

The creation of these farmsteads marks a very persistent centrifugal dispersion of the population, moving outwards from the "town" nucleus, as it rose in numbers. This was only made possible by two conditions, the one physical, the other economic. The alternation of shales and grits ensured a water supply at all levels, so that every homestead possessed a spring or runnel of soft water. Economically these small holdings could provide subsistence for a family, but they could not yield a livelihood. Their purpose was to afford conveniences for the manufacture of cloth , their owners were clothiers engaged in trade, or at least, yeomen and small farmers who kept a loom going in their spare hours. The Elizabethan and Jacobean homesteads in themselves testify to the wealth that trade alone could bring to these Pennine uplands.

Defoe noticed these three correlated facts very acutely as he rode towards Halifax two centuries ago, and he expatiated upon them in a famous passage too long to quote in full.[1]

" Then it was I began to perceive the reason and nature of the thing, and found that this division of the land into small pieces and scattering of the dwellings, was occasioned by, and done for the convenience of the business which the people were generally employed in, . . .

" This business is the clothing trade, for the convenience of which the houses are thus scattered and spread upon the sides of the hills, even from the bottom to the top ; the reason is this : such has been the bounty of nature to this otherwise frightful country, that two things essential to the business, as well as the ease of the people are found here, and that in a situation which I never saw the like of in any part of England ; . . . I mean coals and running water upon the tops of the highest hills. . . .

" I found as our road passed among them, for indeed no road could do otherwise, wherever we passed any house we found a little rill or gutter of running water, if the house was above the road, it came from it and crossed the way to run to another ; if the house was below us, it crossed us from some other distant house above it, and at every considerable house was a manufactory or work-house, and as they could not do their business without water, the little streams were so parted and guided by gutters or pipes, and by turning and dividing the streams, that none of those houses were without a river, if I may call it so, running into and through their work-houses."

What Defoe reveals, and described in further detail, is an industrial population settled upon the land, much thicker than any agricultural population and yet not congregated in towns, nor largely in villages, but dispersed on the hills. Even if Defoe's enthusiasm tempts him to colour the picture too brightly, he paints on his canvas both the domestic industry and its background as he saw them. He has seized upon the significant facts and his picture is true to life. Ample confirmation of the dispersion of the population is to be found, half a century later, in Jefferys' *Map of Yorkshire*, 1771, in which all the hill country from the Calder southwards, from Halifax and Heptonstall to Sheffield and Rotherham and up to Holmfirth and Saddleworth, is crowded with the names of separate houses or clusters of houses, in strong contrast to the bare spaces between the villages elsewhere.

But the " bounty of nature " was not limited to the springs and rills on the hillsides for the washing and dyeing of wool. There were also swift streams in the valley-bottoms that could be dammed to drive water wheels to raise the fulling stocks. Almost from the beginning one stage of the manufacture of cloth, the modern "milling" was carried out in a mill or " myln," which was set up where power

[1] *A Tour through England and Wales*, 1724–26, Everyman Ed. II., pp. 193–195.

could be obtained, and where there was an abundance of soft water for the scouring of the cloth. The early manorial fulling mills might be at what were relatively populous centres, such as Wakefield, Leeds, Dewsbury or Halifax, but after the suppression of the monasteries in the 16th century the new landed gentry and the wealthier clothiers sought for sites further up in the hills, where new fulling mills could be set to serve the neighbouring clothiers, or their own trade. Even ancient fulling mills could be remote from the villages they served, if these, like Almondbury, stood high above the valley bottom. The fulling mill down on the stream might then have nothing but a bridge and the miller's cottage in its vicinity. These Tudor mills created new foci, usually at an existing bridge ; if not, the miller soon put up his own bridge. To these sites other processes gravitated. The fulling miller himself often finished the cloth, for the great shears used for cropping were called " walker shears " showing that they were used at the " walk miln." The supply of water attracted also the cloth or piece dyer. So corn mill, fulling mill and dye-house clustered together at a bridge, sometimes all under the same roof. But the fulling mill often worked only half the year, and none needed more than a man or two, so that these power centres in the valleys remained small scattered units except in the immediate neighbourhood of the market towns.

Then suddenly at the end of the 18th century the embryo began to develop under the stimulus of the Lancashire inventions for carding and spinning cotton. All fulling mills expanded into scribbling mills for the preparatory processes of carding wool ready for the spinners, whilst additional scribbling mills sprang up like mushrooms wherever water power was to be had. From that time the cluster of cottages around a water-mill at a bridge grew rapidly into a populous industrial village with its workers tending machinery, whilst the hill-top " town " of which it was an off-shoot continued to carry on the hand processes. So there rose a stratification in the industry, a horizontal cleavage between the weaving or manufacturing on the hills and the carding and spinning down in the valleys. It was some time before woollen spinning gravitated down into the scribbling mills, but the early cotton spinning mills led the way.

The centre of gravity was shifted, and as it has been aptly said of the Calder valley, " the world was turned upside down." The workers of Sowerby or Heptonstall had lived and worked, as it were, on the top of a dome or inverted bowl. Henceforth they were to live and work in the bottom of a bowl and the towns of Sowerby Bridge and Hebden Bridge to sprawl up the sides towards the old hamlets on its rim. They are only examples of what happened wherever the original focus—a mill and bridge—was at the confluence of two streams and valleys. But even if it did not take this form there was everywhere a pronounced descent. Huddersfield reaped the advantage of being nearer the Colne and the King's Mill, and grew at the expense of Almondbury. Holme threw out off-shoots lower down stream at Holme Bridge and Holmfirth, and on another tributary at the " New Mill " of the 16th century. Meltham gave rise to Meltham Mills and Rastrick to Brighouse. The names alone are suggestive, and doubly so Milnsbridge embodying both elements. At an ancient crossing of the Colne and the convergence of narrow valleys the mill was well placed to serve several upland townships. There is another aspect of this descent. The multiplication of mills along the streams began a ribbon development of the valleys that has produced one of the most familiar and most characteristic features of the industrial Pennines. Streams played the first part in this, but canals, turnpike roads and railways all in turn contributed to the congestion of the narrow valleys which they penetrated. Canals and railways were of necessity bound to make use of valleys as far as possible, and when first one and then the other tunnelled through the watershed, the Colne Valley and the Tame were converted from blind alleys into a through corridor. The part played by roads is much less obvious than the others they may be of any age. Comparison of the modern map with Jefferys' map of 1771 or Warburton's of 1720 will, however, show that a new system of main roads was evolved by the turnpike trusts. It is not easy to name a town or village in the neighbourhood of Huddersfield that is served to-day by the road in use two centuries ago. Parts of the older road may be retained, but again and again diversions have been made to secure easier gradients, or more direct routes constructed. Above all, the turnpike road gradually worked its way down off the spurs and hill tops into the valleys, which earlier highways had avoided. The first turnpike to Stanedge and Manchester followed the old highway high on the valley flanks and only came down to the Colne at Marsden, to leave it at once. The later one follows the valley the whole way, though hardly ever getting down into the bottom, like the canal which preceded it. The valley floor was too narrow for both.

While all these forces worked together to crowd an industrial population into the valleys the uplands saw little change. The output of the scribbling mills came up to the villages to be spun on the jenny and to be woven on the handloom, and even when spinning went to the mills the villages continued to be full of clothiers and handloom weavers. Ultimately, if there was coal to he had near at hand, the clothier who was employing many handloom weavers built a mill near his warehouse and introduced power looms. It was the natural course, for his weavers were all round about on the uplands. It was not always a permanent success, for circumstances varied and conditions changed, but in most upland villages the tradition of weaving has never been broken. Cloth is manufactured in great mills that have grown out of the domestic premises of the clothier and are often owned by lineal descendants. They may now be spinners as well, though worsted has usually retained the separation of the processes. But manufacturing, i.e., weaving, could only survive on the hills and in the old hill-top towns if coal could be obtained locally, or could be brought economically. The little mills, run by the wholly inadequate water-power of some moorland stream, supplemented perhaps by the coal won from a thin seam outcropping on the hill side, had their day. Their ruins are to be seen in the sequestered cloughs and on the moor edge both in Lancashire and Yorkshire, and they mark the transition from a domestic industry to modern industrial conditions.

So the ordinary traveller, whether by rail or road, sees little of the older industrialism that lies above him on the hills. He may penetrate the Pennines from Wakefield up the Calder valley to Burnley or Rochdale, or from Huddersfield to Stockport by the Colne and the Tame. It will be wool or worsted or cotton all the way, and the ribbon of modern industry will unroll before his eyes in an unbroken chain. But if he would seek out the older hill roads that link these places he would often be above it all and often back in the 17th or 18th century ; and yet he would see that the hills have their place in the modern world of industry, besides being the seat of the older domestic industry.

COAL.

The arrival of the steam engine ended the dominancy of the streams. Coal at last became the decisive factor in the progress of the industry. For half a century or more it depended upon local supplies, so that nearness to a pit, or at least to a canal, determined the success of many an enterprise. Huddersfield was well placed, for two of its valleys were on or adjacent to the coal field, and the third, the Colne valley, which traversed the belt of Millstone Grits, was fed by a canal.

Yet the Grits were not devoid of coal seams, and one, the Upper Meltham Coal with its fireclay, had been and is of importance locally. Others are much too thin for profitable working, but in the early days of the steam engine when it was used to supplement water power, they were drawn upon for engine coal by day holes or shallow pits. Isolated mills dependent upon such inadequate supplies could only have a brief life, and they stand derelict in the remote Deanhead valley telling of the time when coal was won out of the sides of the valley or high up on Pole Moor.

Even the beds in the Lower Coal Measures were relatively thin compared with the rich seams worked in the modern colliery districts, but there was the advantage that they were accessible as they outcropped on the hill sides. The consequence was that coal had been dug from early times and coal mining was an established industry in the district long before the advent of the steam engine. Dr. Wray has described its rise in a previous handbook,[1] and the story of its development in the Huddersfield district is only an example of what was taking place elsewhere along the escarpment of the Lower Coal Measures, especially northwards at Halifax and Bradford. Defoe recognised the value of coal to the textile industry even in his day, when it was used for heating the dye vats. Probably he had Halifax in his mind when he thought that one reason for having the pits on the hill tops was " because the horses which fetch the coals go light

[1] *The Mining Industry in the Huddersfield District*, Tolson Memorial Museum Handbook VI.

up the hills and come loaden down " ; but it was a familiar sight long after his time in the Huddersfield district as well.

The fact was that throughout the 17th and 18th centuries coal had been won in increasing quantities right in the heart of the Yorkshire woollen district, adding to its wealth and promoting its industries, so that when the steam engine caused a rapid rise in the demand it was met instantly and on the spot. Literally so sometimes, for the outcrops were known and a mill might be placed where the coal could be got and conveyed straight into the boiler-house, as at Linfits near Kirkburton. The scribbling mills were already tied to the streams, but coal and steam enabled weaving to remain on the uplands as the power loom did not come before 1830. Many upland villages felt the benefit, and at least one (Queensbury) came into existence for no other reason ; and the coal there is truly on the hill top, for Queensbury stands 1,100 feet above sea level. Round Huddersfield the distribution of the "fancy" trade seems to be due to the stimulus of coal, as it was restricted to the Coal Measures throughout the first half of the last century. The power loom, however, was not the primary cause of this distribution, but rather the use of steam power in a "factory," which was both a scribbling mill and a manufacturing centre, with handlooms within its walls.

So, with the advantages of early development, of easy winning at no great depth and of a local demand, coal-mining in the district expanded rapidly in the nineteenth century until the 'seventies. As late as 1871 the Bradford area had fifty collieries raising nearly two million tons of coal, though scarcely one survives to-day. Dr. Wray states that at the beginning of the century there were twenty pits working between Huddersfield and Holmfirth ; and the larger area around Halifax, Dewsbury, Huddersfield and Holmfirth was producing a quarter of the Yorkshire output by 1860. No one would call it a colliery district to-day, for as the profitable seams in the Lower Coal Measures become exhausted coal-mining moved eastwards. But the woollen industry showed no tendency to follow it in its migration, for one reason, because railways had by that time become a distributing medium.

The Lower Coal Measures have, therefore, been a great asset in the economic life of the woollen district, just as their escarpment has been a prominent feature of the landscape. It forms the immediate background to the town of Halifax, which lies on the Rough Rock at the very foot of the bold scarp that sweeps down from the heights of Denholme and Queensbury to swing round Halifax and pass on to cross the Calder at Elland, with a stream at its base the whole way. The hill-side is built up of a succession of shales, sandstones, fireclays, bands of nodular ironstones and coal seams, culminating in the massive Elland Flagstones at the top. It is an epitome of the Lower Coal Measures, and its mineral wealth from base to summit has been exploited for many centuries. The Soft Bed and the Hard Bed are the two most important coal-seams, either for themselves or the associated minerals.

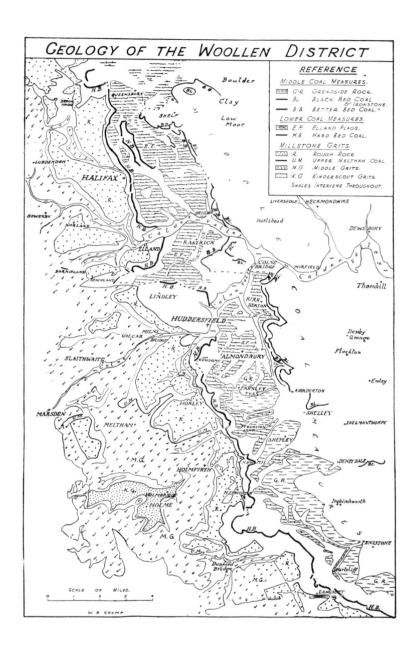

GEOLOGY OF THE WOOLLEN DISTRICT

REFERENCE

MIDDLE COAL MEASURES.
G.R. GRENOSIDE ROCK.
B.L. BLACK BED COAL & IRONSTONE.
B.B. BETTER BED COAL.

LOWER COAL MEASURES.
E.F. ELLAND FLAGS.
H.B. HARD BED COAL.

MILLSTONE GRITS.
R. ROUGH ROCK.
U.M. UPPER MELTHAM COAL.
M.G. MIDDLE GRITS.
K.G. KINDERSCOUT GRITS.
SHALES INTERVENE THROUGHOUT.

At Huddersfield the arrangement is not quite so simple. The Rough Rock is further away on Lindley Moor and along Longwood Edge, whilst the town stands on the Soft Bed Flags or other rocks below the Hard Bed coal. Immediately to the south of the town the river Colne cuts through the Rough Rock in a narrow gorge at Paddock, and from that point the tributary Holme practically separates the Rough Rock from the Lower Coal Measures. Once more the complete succession reappears as a bold escarpment forming the eastern flank of the valley and running southwards from Berry Brow to Thurstonland, Holmfirth and Hepworth. In Almondbury it rises in a series of terraces that culminate in flat-topped summits of Elland Flags that extend northwards through Dalton Bank to Colne Bridge (see Fig. 2).

Then beyond the belt of Elland Flags there rises another escarpment, behind which lies mainly a colliery district. From Shelf to Brighouse and from Colne Bridge to Kirkburton and Shepley this escarpment is accentuated by the streams flowing at its base, and along the eastern slopes of these valleys the outcrops of its two famous seams, the Better Bed and the Black Bed, have been worked for the benefit of the textile industry in a similar way to the Soft Bed and the Hard Bed. The textile area in fact definitely includes their outcrops, which are marked by a chain of early mills and older warehouses and dyehouses. Immediately above the Black Bed coal comes the Grenoside Rock, which forms a prominent plateau at Highburton and across the valley in Farnley Tyas, and it caps Castle Hill as well.[2]

IRON.

This escarpment has contributed something more than coal to promote the prosperity of the textile industry and to establish it in earlier centuries. Southwards from Bradford to Bradley and Colne Bridge there are shales containing nodules and layers of ironstone immediately above the Black Bed, in place of the Grenoside Rock. Smelted by coke from the Better Bed coal of exceptional purity, this ironstone has produced the famous Low Moor iron from the end of the 18th century until recent years. The group of furnaces, forges

[2] Dr. Wray, who was engaged on the recent geological resurvey of this district, has given reasons (*Proceedings Yorks. Geological Soc.* 1929) for regarding the Elland Flags as the summit of the Lower Coal Measures, and the Better Bed as the beginning of the Middle Coal Measures. These turn upon the identification of the Better Bed of Yorkshire with the Arley Mine in Lancashire, which is taken as the base of the Middle Coal Measures in the Lancashire Coalfield. The Geological Survey has, however, retained the older dividing line of the Blocking or Silkstone Coal, although admitting in its Memoir, *The Country around Huddersfield and Halifax* 1930, that the Better Bed "would probably make a more suitable line of sub-division." Of its advantage in this district there can be no doubt, because the Elland Flagstones form a most prominent horizon, putting the crown to a series of rocks that form one escarpment. But there is a greater reason. When the Arley Mine is identified with the Better Bed, it is apparent for the first time that the cotton towns of Lancashire which were formerly engaged in the woollen industry have exactly the same geological setting as the Yorkshire textile towns.

and foundries around Low Moor played no small part in fostering the wool-textile industry in the early days of machinery and the steam engine. But the industry has always had need of iron and iron workers to provide it with its tools ; and it is not yet realised how greatly the presence of iron ore in the Coal Measures has promoted the industry in the Pennines, and how wide spread iron working has been at one time or another. Before coke could be used the woods of the Pennines from Hallamshire to the Forest of Knaresborough were being exploited to smelt iron mined near at hand.

Dr. Wray has described the medieval ironstone mining of this district in his Museum Handbook and has noted that Fountains Abbey had a forge in Bradley Wood, and mined the Black Bed iron-stone at or near Colne Bridge. More recently Mr. J. Walton has found a bloomery, with the scoriæ or " cinders " all round it, within Bradley Wood, and concludes that the nodules above the Better Bed were used in this case. Medieval workings, however, are only a starting point, though in fact Fountains Abbey went so far in the development of its estates here as to throw bridges across both the Colne and the Calder early in the 13th century on the sites of Colne Bridge and Cooper Bridge.

More important is the further fact mentioned by Dr. Wray that Colne Bridge had ironworks producing on an average 150 tons of iron annually in the 18th century. The authority for this is to be found in two lists of Yorkshire Forges quoted by Dr. Maud Sellers in the *Victoria County History* (Vol. II., p. 387), where Colne Bridge is credited with 140 tons both before and in 1725, and 150 tons in 1746. Nothing else was known about the Forge until Mr. Legh Tolson issued in 1929 his sumptuous and privately published volume on the *History of the Church of St. John the Baptist, Kirkheaton,* in which he traces the succession of ironmasters from Thomas Beaumont, who died in 1560, to Charles Brook, who in July, 1776, watched his men " rolling hoops, the first that were ever rolled at Colne Bridge." Yet Thomas Dickens, an earlier master (1623–1692), had invented a rolling mill, for Thoresby saw at Kirkstall Forge before 1715 " a mill that Mr. Dickens of late years erected for rolling Iron into plates and bars." It is hardly necessary to follow the fortunes of these vanished ironworks further, though Mr. Walton has found the site of the forge close to Colne Bridge. The point of importance is that here was a supply of native iron, possibly of the high quality of Low Moor iron, right in the heart of the woollen area, two centuries before iron-smelting is heard of in the Low Moor district ; though it is likely that iron was being produced in that neighbourhood a good deal earlier than Bradford historians state.

Reference has already been made to the presence in medieval York of wire-drawers and card-makers who supplied the woollen workers with one of their essential tools—the hand-cards or wire brushes used for carding wool preparatory to spinning. In the 17th century Barnsley specialised in wire-drawing, for it was near the

South Yorkshire ironworks ; but the industry declined there, undoubtedly because there was a rival in the field better placed to meet the demand. Card-makers certainly make their appearance at Halifax and Brighouse in the 17th century, and long before the introduction of machinery wire-drawing and card-making were twin industries firmly established in a limited area either side of the line of outcrop of the Black Band ironstone. Carding by machinery brought a great expansion and a multiplication of makers without extending the area. Both Low Moor and Colne Bridge were then producing iron, and the trade was concentrated round these two foci, at Scholes and Cleckheaton in the north, and at Mirfield, Brighouse, Liversedge and, later, Lindley, round Colne Bridge in the south, whilst Halifax was in touch with either. Yet the cause of this distribution has never been perceived, in a great measure because there was no evidence of a local supply of iron.

There can be little doubt but that Low Moor continued to nurture this local trade during the 19th century as long as the industry used forge-iron or wrought-iron for its wire staples. From the start it seems to have had a large share of the immense demand for the cotton industry. In 1825 there were as many card-makers in either of the villages of Clifton or Hightown as in all Lancashire, and fifty years later probably nine-tenths of the card-clothing required for the world's textile machinery was made in this district. A local supply of iron now counts for nothing, but historic continuity counts for a good deal. Many of the existing firms trace their descent from the card-makers of the 18th century, and the industry is still concentrated in the same area within four miles of Brighouse. It is, however, a sign of the times that the English Card Clothing Company has recently opened a manufacturing branch in Japan, to save its trade in the Far East.

There are other examples of the service of iron to the woollen industry. Some parts of the loom and wheels in the clothier's shop and of the fulling stocks at the mill had always to be wrought at the village smithy. But the only other specialised craft was that of the shears maker, for it was beyond the skill of the ordinary smith. Very little is known of it except that it was a distinct craft in the Calder valley before the end of the 16th century and continued until little more than a century ago.

The 19th century with the introduction of machinery brought a great increase in the consumption of iron, and the jobbing smith developed into mechanic and eventually into machine-maker. Many textile towns can supply examples of the transition and of the rise of engineering trades subsidiary to the staple industry, though chance has played a considerable part in their distribution. Iron and coal, within limits, have been invaluable allies, but modern collieries, steel works and engineering shops do not assimilate with woollen and worsted mills. Sheffield and Rotherham have quite definitely ousted the woollen industry from the valleys of the Dearne and the Don.

Skelmanthorpe on the watershed with Denby Dale and Scissett lower down are now the outposts of the Huddersfield trade in the one. In the other, Plumpton Mill in Thurlstone, where Thomas Tomasson & Son have been manufacturers of livery cloths for over a century, is all that remains of the warehouses and mills that were to be found on the hills and on the streams around Penistone. Its Cloth Hall, built in 1763, still stands, but is converted into shops.

Apart from the geographical advantage of site the initial element in the rise of a Pennine "clothing" town has been the possession of a church, followed by the creation of a market. A parish church implied a parish—a territory of which the church town was capital. The mineral wealth of the Lower Coal Measures was still latent, and in this respect it was an accident that all these ancient churches nearest the hills were placed on or so close to the Lower Coal Measures that every one of them reaped the benefit of the hidden wealth, and found in it another real cause of industrial prosperity.

But an earlier asset was the magnitude of their territory. As a rule their parishes ran right up into the hills, and this wide area over the Millstone Grits, useless for all else, fed the market town with the cloth that it wove. Halifax is a perfect illustration of the advantage, for with a parish that extended fifteen miles each way it had a very large and relatively populous area to draw upon without any rivalry, although two daughter churches were almost independent ecclesiastically. Indeed in its palmiest days cloth came to its Piece Hall from far beyond the limits of the parish. In Whalley parish, the other side of the Pennines, the same principles worked out a totally different result. The parish was excessively large, and Whalley at the furthest end had no contact with the Lower Coal Measures and no share in the industry. On the contrary Burnley and Colne, ancient chapelries within the parish, were well placed on or close to the Coal Measures, with a measure of Grit country adjacent, and so achieved the position of market or clothing towns, whilst Whalley still remains a village.

In the Huddersfield district the vigour of Christianity in the Calder valley before the Conquest produced a number of smaller parishes along that border. Nor were the two largest, though they ran up into the hills, comparable with Halifax in size. The churches of Almondbury and Huddersfield were both on the Lower Coal Measures and Almondbury had a cloth market at an early date. Yet of the two, Huddersfield was the more favourably situated and gradually ousted Almondbury after it had obtained market rights in 1671. Still there was need of more territory to feed a Cloth Hall, and overriding parish boundaries Huddersfield established itself as the market centre for the whole of the Colne basin, or four parishes in all. Saddleworth also, in spite of being over the watershed, and in the parish of Rochdale, brought all its cloth to Huddersfield as long as it wove woollens by hand. Now it turns to Manchester, but Huddersfield still dominates its own natural region, the basin of the Colne and its tributaries.

CHAPTER III.

THE RISE OF THE INDUSTRY, 1300-1500.

The history of the woollen industry in the Huddersfield district begins with the establishment of a weekly market at Almondbury in the year 1294. The grant of this was made to Henry Lacy (or de Lascy) the famous Earl of Lincoln, who held the larger portion of the district as part of his great Honour of Pontefract. Beyond the Pennines he was lord of the Honour of Clitheroe and the lands that became the Duchy of Lancaster. The Earl was an able administrator and stimulated the development of the natural resources of his estates. One sign of his progressive policy is the licence that he obtained from Edward I. to hold weekly markets and annual fairs not only at Almondbury, but at Pontefract, Bradford and Burnley. Taking into consideration the fulling mills that existed during his lifetime at Colne, Bradford and Burnley, it seems likely that Almondbury also possessed one, though there is no definite mention of it for another half century.

Then in 1340 a survey of the manor shows the existence in Almondbury of a water corn-mill, a fulling mill let at 13s. and a dye-house at 6s. 8d. annually. No clue is given as to their position, but the mills would be on the site of the existing King's mills on the Colne. It is also evident that the mills served Huddersfield as well as Almondbury, and from their position they came to be called Huddersfield Mills. Later, when through John of Gaunt the estates of the Duchy of Lancaster passed to the Crown, the manorial mills became known as the King's Mills. So in 1584, when Queen Elizabeth ordered a survey of her manor of Almondbury, the bounds were found to follow " the water of Colne as it descendeth to the Queen's Majesty's Mills, named in the records Huddersfield Mills." These then comprised a water corn-mill and a fulling mill " annexed to the corn-mill and lately rebuilt by William Ramsden, the farmer of the corn-mill as the former one on the tail-goit had fallen into utter decay.[1]

Returning to the 13th century, there are other records that reveal the presence of fullers and dyers in the Huddersfield district, as well as a string of fulling mills down the Calder about the year 1300. In 1297 Edward I. was granted a lay subsidy of a ninth on the goods of the " respectable men " of the realm.[2] The rolls that have survived relating to Yorkshire give individual details for the whole of the wapentake of Agbrigg, and thus present the earliest economic survey of the Huddersfield district, at least the first that dealt with wealth in the form of personal property and not land. Everything was on a very modest scale ; the townships around Huddersfield only had half a dozen residents in each liable to be taxed, for the peasantry were exempt. Some of them were named according to their occupation, and amongst these was John the Dyer (Tynctor) of Almondbury, who

[1] *Almondbury in Feudal Times*, J. K. Walker, *Yorks. Arch. Journ.* II. (1871), pp. 1-34.
[2] *Yorkshire Lay Subsidy*, 25 Edw. I., Yorks. Record Series XVI.

was taxed on one ox, one cow, one horse and two quarters of oats of a total value of 14s. At Farnley there was a Ralph the Fuller and at Flocton a Mercer. Here then there is clear evidence contemporary with the new market at Almondbury of fulling and dyeing.

Some parts of the district, Kirkburton, Holmfirth, Shepley and Shelley, with much of the Calder valley, were in the great manor of Wakefield, of which the court rolls are preserved from the year 1274. The earlier rolls have been published [1] and afford a microscopic picture of the economic and social conditions. Certainly there were fulling mills before or soon after 1300 at Sowerby (bridge), Halifax, Brighouse, Mirfield, Dewsbury and Wakefield. When the Court was held at Kirkburton, as it was regularly, the proceedings reveal facts touching the Huddersfield district very closely. In 1315 there is a " William the Fuller " at Holme, and next year " John Fuller or Walker of Gouthelakkers " is named. He evidently was known by either name, and as he lived in Golcar his little "walk-miln" must have been just above Milnsbridge, and probably was a part of the manorial corn-mill from which the bridge derived its name. About the same time there is mention of " John the Walker of Emmeley," and of " Gilbert the Litster of Byrton," i.e., Kirkburton.

These names prove that the cloth manufacture was established in the district from the early years of Edward I., but they do not prove that there was a market for the cloth. It may have been wholly for local consumption, though the springing up of markets and fairs all around after 1250 suggests that a regular trade in cloth began about the same time.

At so early a date it is not probable that cloth was woven from any but home-grown wool, and the Subsidy of 1297 offers proof that sheep were being raised in the district on a small scale. So " Ralph the Fuller " in Farnley, already named, appears as the owner of eight sheep, whilst Francis Tyas, the largest landowner, paid tax on ten sheep, valued as usual at sixpence each. Two other Farnley men raise the total to twenty-five. Only one local township, Shitlington, had a greater number (31), and others dwindled down from Lepton 16, Burton 16, Whitley 14, Holmfirth 14, Quarmby 12, to none in Almondbury, Dalton and Honley. In all, the wapentake of Agbrigg only accounted for 220 sheep, or just one-tenth of the total for the West Riding (exclusive of monastic sheep).

The numbers do not prove much in the way of wool production, but the Subsidy does not cover the whole ground, for the peasantry escaped tax entirely and the clergy were also exempt. Other sources, especially the court rolls of the manor of Wakefield, that record the petty crimes of the day, give a truer insight even if it is less systematic. Sheep were often a matter of dispute, and the people concerned were the cottagers, or peasantry. Thus, in 1298 a Farnley man complained that he had paid three half-pence for the winter keep of a wether to John of Holme, who at shearing time refused to hand over the fleece to him. The same John of Holme was charged the

---

[1] *Court Rolls of the Manor of Wakefield*, Vols. I.–IV., Yorks. Record Series.

previous year with pasturing his sheep in his neighbour's corn, and with breaking a bargain to sell two stones of wool for 7s. Another complaint in 1297 related to thirty-four milch ewes carried off from the common fields of Shelley to Cumberworth Moor and there milked.

Another example from Holme appears to reveal an attempt to evade the tax and deceive the collectors by a trick that has its modern counterpart. Richard of the Grene in Holmfirth was assessed for the subsidy upon two oxen, two cows, one horse and six quarters of oats, of a total value of 19s. 6d. He was in fact a man of wealth, though this was not the sum of it ; for the Wakefield Court Rolls show that Richard of the Grene was ordered a few months earlier to find sureties that " he will not remove his goods, viz., 3 oxen, 3 cows, 24 sheep and 10 qrs. of oats, from the Earl's fee," *i.e.*, out of Holme to, say, Cumberworth Moor. At any rate the sheep had disappeared when the collectors called.

In the middle of the 14th century the Black Death swept the country and brought many economic changes in its train. But in the Pennine hills, where there were no labour problems because the great manors had no demesne arable land to be ploughed by the peasants, the choice between tillage and sheep-pasture did not arise. Life, in fact, went on as before. The Returns of the Poll Tax of 1379 illuminate the century with a searching light that reveals in some measure the distribution, the wealth and the occupations of the population. The Poll Tax was a head tax, laid upon everybody, except the clergy, children and mendicants or paupers, and graded according to their rank. An earl paid four pounds, a peasant four pence, equivalent to four days' wages, though husband and wife counted as one only. Every one was entered on the Rolls by name, and usually his occupation or rank was stated unless he paid only fourpence. Even then his name may indicate his employment : he may be called " Webster" or " Schepehird," " Bateman," *i.e.*, employed by Bate the Lister, or " John servant of Boteler," who kept the inn. But though it is the least in evidence it was the land that claimed the toil of the vast majority of the peasantry, ploughing their half-acres in the village fields as described by the contemporary Piers Plowman.

The Returns compel at once a readjustment of values. The future woollen district was then almost the least populous and the least wealthy area in the West Riding. Even Wakefield and Leeds were outstripped by such little market towns as Tickhill and Snaith. Greater population and wealth were to be found consistently to the south and the east.

Looking at the Huddersfield district in particular,[1] Almondbury, though then a market town in name, could only number about twenty households and little more than a hundred people within its borders. No one paid more than the minimum tax, except the smith and the wheelwright, who contributed sixpence. That represents the average township of the district ; Halifax was certainly no larger or wealthier. Above these came in ascending order, Dewsbury, Hudders-

---

[1] Details are to be found in the local histories.

field, Thornhill, Elland and Mirfield, with about double the population and a sprinkling of residents of some rank or importance. Saddleworth also had about two hundred inhabitants, widely scattered among the hills ; and the extensive area under Holmfirth numbered some eighty families or four hundred people, similarly scattered, and without a hint of trade.

It is clearly impossible that at this time the output of cloth from either the Huddersfield district, or the wider one that included Wakefield and Leeds, could have been large or comparable with the production of York and the towns. The disparity in population and wealth was too great to admit of competition. Yet the Poll Tax Returns reveal the presence of cloth workers of various grades. Elland had two merchants and a webster, whilst three people went by the name of Lister and one Walker. Under the name of "Willelmus Shalunhare" is hidden a coverlet weaver, or "chaloner," more usual in the older centres. Websters were to be found in Thornhill, Flockton and Thurstonland, and a merchant at Huddersfield. Nowhere in the district does anyone appear as a fuller in the list of occupations ; but as a name the equivalent "Walker" occurs quite frequently, as in Almondbury, Honley (2), South Crosland (2), Mirfield and Kirkburton (3). Some of them were undoubtedly walkers by trade as well as by name, but as all of them fell within the lowest rank their occupation was not stated.

So, with these scraps of evidence as proof of its existence the cloth manufacture of the district may be left to grow up during the next century whilst we look at what was happening outside. One of the first signs of state control of the industry was the appointment of an official to measure all cloth offered for sale and to affix his leaden seal to the piece if it was of proper (assize) length and breadth, or otherwise to confiscate it. His fee, called "ulnage," was a halfpenny, and he was the Ulnager or Aulnager. As the State was supervising the production of cloth, it was an easy step to obtain a revenue from it, and in 1353 Edward III., famous for his encouragement of the manufacture, obtained from Parliament the grant of a subsidy of four pence on each cloth of assize offered for sale. This the ulnagers also collected when they attached their seals. A half cloth paid half the subsidy, but any cloths less than half the standard cloth of assize (26 yds.) escaped altogether.

The cloths woven in the West Riding, i.e., in the hills, were cheap coarse stuffs, only half the length and half the width of the town product, and being only a quarter of a cloth of assize they escaped the subsidy. This is apparent from the description of them as strait (narrow) cloths and "northern dozens" (12 yds. in length), though the most famous of the narrow woollen cloths was the "kersey" or "carsay," which derived its name from Kersey, a beautiful one-street village in the south of Suffolk. The exemption of the West Riding cloths came to an end in 1393 when the law was amended to allow any weaver to "make and put to sale cloths, as well Kerseys as others, of such length and breadth as him shall please," provided he paid subsidy thereon *pro rata.* So henceforth every kersey woven in the West Riding for the next three centuries contributed a penny to the Exchequer, and the clothiers stubbornly fought every attempt to make them pay more.

The late Mr. John Lister of Shibden Hall, Halifax, fifty years ago discovered the surviving Ulnagers' Rolls in the Public Record Office and these rolls have thrown more light on the early history of the industry than any other document.[1] The early rolls, e.g., in 1395–6, gather the names of the West Riding producers under market centres, such as Wakefield 173 cloths, Pontefract 105 cloths, Leeds 120 cloths, Ripon 168 cloths, and closer analysis is difficult. All that need be said is that the total output of the West Riding was only one-fifth that of York.

Then there comes a long gap in the Rolls. When they recommence they show a great change in progress, for the West Riding is producing as much as York, and Halifax is challenging Ripon for first place in the Riding. Almondbury also is making headway, so that for two years, 1473–75, the order of the West Riding centres runs thus : Halifax 1,493 cloths, Ripon 1,386, Almondbury 427, Leeds 320, Pontefract 214, Bradford 178, Wakefield 160 and Barnsley 142. It must be understood that a cloth means a whole cloth which paid 4d., or its equivalent, i.e., four kerseys, so that the figures must be multiplied by four to obtain the number of pieces sealed at Halifax and Almondbury in two years.

There remains to be gleaned from the Ulnagers' Rolls something more about the industry in Almondbury. In the earlier Rolls individual clothiers are named, but in these later ones there is only a summary, prefixed by one or two names, presumably of responsible merchants who served as sponsors of their town's cloths. Mr. Lister has in fact shown that for Doncaster and Barnsley these sponsors were men of mark or of well-known families. The first mention of Almondbury is in the account of Thomas Treygott for 1469–70, and is in this form :

> Robert Nevyl, of Almondebury, subsidy and ulnage of 160 cloths sealed there. 60s.

In Ralph Byrand's account for 1471–73 the entry runs :

> John Nevell, Thomas Bemand, Laurence Key, and the other men of the Town of Almondesbury, for 320 cloths there sealed during the time aforesaid. Subsidy and Ulnage £6.

Here then are the names of four men who attested the cloths brought to the Almondbury cloth market, and who therefore must have been accustomed to frequent the market. Probably they were what we should now call prominent merchants, though they called themselves "clothiers." Who were they ? As soon as the disguise of the ancient spelling is penetrated two of them are seen to bear names

---

[1] They are now published in full in *The Early Yorkshire Woollen Trade,* edited by J. Lister. Y.A.S. Record Series, Vol. 64 1924.

that have ranked for centuries amongst the most honoured and distinguished in the district, viz., Beaumont of Whitley Beaumont, and Kaye of Woodsome Hall. Thomas Bemand is the name most easily identified, for he can hardly be anybody but Thomas Beaumont of Whitley Beaumont, who succeeded to the estates in 1469, and on his death in 1495 was buried in Kirkheaton Church. He also provides a clue to Robert Nevyl, for in 1456 he had married Elizabeth, daughter of Robert Nevile of Liversedge. Moreover, his father Richard Beaumont appointed the same Robert Nevile as one of the supervisors of his will made in 1469. The Neviles of Liversedge were quite as distinguished a family and quite as ancient as the Beaumonts of Whitley. This Robert was the son and heir of Sir Thomas Nevile, who died in 1438, but whose widow was still living at the date of these accounts.

John Nevell, of the second account, was the son of Robert Nevile and brother-in-law of Thomas Beaumont. A business transaction of almost contemporary date shows them playing the part of local gentry with interests in the district. This was a grant in 1468 by Robert Nevill along with John Eland and another of three-quarters of the manor of Hipperholme, otherwise Brighouse, including the mill of Brighouse, to Robert Eland, "John Nevill son of Robert Nevill" and others. John Nevile in later years received a knighthood and was High Sheriff of Yorkshire. Laurence Key is more difficult to identify. Besides the Kays or Cays of Woodsome Hall, there were by this time branches of the family established elsewhere in Almondbury and the neighbourhood, and all that can be said is that Laurence was one of the family and probably the one named in a deed of 1485-6,[1] to which Edmund Cay (perhaps of Thorpe) and William Cay of Farnley were parties and John Cay of Woodsome a witness. He is there described as " Laurence Cay of Almondbury."[2]

So Almondbury emerges into the light at the end of the Middle Ages as the seat of a flourishing little cloth market drawing its supplies from a fairly wide district. So much stress has been laid upon the domestic character of the Pennine industry and the multitude of its little clothiers, that it comes as a surprise to find the most distinguished families of the district figuring in the cloth trade. But why not ? Wool and cloth were then the great sources of wealth. and there was nothing derogatory in trade. It was the very time when churches were being rebuilt and enlarged and the great Perpendicular churches of Suffolk and the Cotswolds, of Halifax, Wakefield and Almondbury itself owe their magnificence to clothiers and merchants who lavished their wealth upon their adornment. The clothing town or village might be small and mean, but its church must be great and glorious,

[1] *Yorkshire Deeds* V., under Almondbury. Y.A.S. Record Series.

[2] The name occurs again in the 1533 list of Almondbury clothiers (see p. 41) as " Laurence Kay of Almbrige," apparently an error in copying for " Almbrye."

CHAPTER IV.

THE YEOMAN-CLOTHIER : HIS TOOLS AND HIS TRADE 1500-1700.

The gradual rise of the cloth industry in the district described in the last chapter covered a period of two hundred years. For the next two centuries 1500–1700 the development and organisation of the industry continued on the same lines. The central figure was always the clothier and all the processes save the fulling were carried on in domestic premises. Nowhere does the accepted title of the Domestic System suit the organisation of the industry so well as in the West Riding, for here the master clothier was in the main only master of his own household, and nearly every householder was a clothier. Of course households were not of equal size, and the clothier in a bigger way might well have one or two apprentices working in his "shop," but the journeyman was practically non-existent. Even in the 18th century the village weaver owned his own loom and wove at home, though his material was supplied by the master clothier, and the pieces returned to him.

The other outstanding feature of the industry was that it was rural. It created a yeoman class that lived on the land, but grew wealthy from the pursuit of trade At first weaving had been a subsidiary occupation, but it rapidly became the mainstay of the growing population. Nearly every yeoman, big or little, became a clothier, but continued to cultivate his small holding for the subsistence of his family. This was only possible by a complete break with medieval conditions. The common-field system of land tenure and cultivation disappeared in the 16th century for all practical purposes in most of the townships. The complementary phase of the change was a continuous settlement of individuals upon the "wastes" or uncultivated lands around and beyond the old ' town." Being granted leave to "intake" an acre or half-an-acre from the waste, a man proceeded to clear it and cultivate it, add to the area by successive grants and erect a homestead on his clearing. In this way the growing population colonised the remoter moorland valleys and the uplands of the townships. Running water or springs were to be found almost everywhere, peat for fuel was always near to hand, the land would grow oats and support a cow or two, and the loom provided a livelihood.

This process was repeated in hundreds of places within the part of the Pennines where weaving flourished, and it was the process by which an industrial population arose. Naturally it did not proceed everywhere exactly on these lines. Some townships had little moorland, in others the manorial lord retained the older system so far as he could, and discouraged individual settlement. So the change might be delayed until late in the 18th century, when the process was different and produced rather an industrial population aggregated in clusters of cottages or folds and divorced or nearly so from the land, though not yet crowded into towns.

Some knowledge of the processes by which wool was manufactured into cloth, of the organisation of the industry in this district, and of its regulation by the State is necessary to build up a picture of the industry during these two centuries. Questions may be asked to which there is no direct answer, but on the whole by aid of local wills, lawsuits and other legal documents, supplemented by Parliamentary Acts and Reports of one kind or another, an adequate representation of the industry may be drawn as it flourished any time between 1500 and 1700. More than once it will be necessary to quote statements and documents relating to Halifax, because the Huddersfield district was engaged in making the same kind of woollen cloth as that in which Halifax had taken the lead in the 15th century, namely the kersey or carsey.

The kersey derived its name from a village in Suffolk (that in Saxton's map is written "Carsey"), where it was being made as early as 1262, from Spanish wool, i.e., wool of good quality. It had a very long vogue as a cheap woollen cloth, particularly favoured for the old style stockings or full-hose, "fine carsie hosen" (1577), which "were kersie to the calf and t'other knit" (1607). A later description, 1724, has it :

> Her stockings were of Kersey green
> As tight as ony silk.

The Suffolk industry began to decay in the 16th century as the West Riding advanced, and it was undoubtedly Halifax, and Huddersfield with it, that then made the kersey a familiar cloth over all Western Europe. It was mentioned by name by a Halifax clothier who left his son "13 white carsies" in 1528 ; and two centuries later Defoe noted the "market for kersies every Tuesday" at Huddersfield and the prodigious increase in the output around Halifax stimulated by "the great demand of their kersies for clothing the armies abroad."

The kersey was a narrow cloth, only a yard in width, and according to an Act of 1552 (for the State in Tudor times was continually regulating the industry) the length was to be 17–18 yards and the weight twenty pounds. Leeds on the contrary made a "broad cloth," 24 yds. by $1\frac{3}{4}$ yds., or "northern dozens" of half the length, so that the kersey was the distinctive product of the upper Calder valley. Southwards round Barnsley and Penistone a coarser cloth known as Pennistones was chiefly made.

There is a brief extract from "A Memorandum Book" written in 1588 and published in the Kenyon MSS. (*Hist. MSS. Comm.*. 108–9) that throws considerable light on the manufacture of kerseys and broad cloth as carried on at Halifax and Leeds respectively. Apparently it is concerned with a proposal to establish the industry in or near Skipton, and is the answer to an enquiry addressed to the Vicar of Leeds, as one who if not versed in the mystery of cloth making, was at least in touch with those who were. It begins abruptly : "The Vycare of Leedes sent for Rauf Mathewe, who ys very skilfull in all things apperteyninge to his trade of clothinge," and proceeds at once to his report : "Instruments : wheels cardes, combes leades, swinginge (rods), comb stocks, loomes, sheares, handles, tassells, tenters."

Then the skilful Ralph draws up a scheme for three score persons to be apportioned to the production of two "dossens" or one "whole cloth" from six stones of undressed wool "after the use of Leades where only brode clothe is made." The details of the alternative scheme for weaving kerseys then follow :

" Three score persons are thus to be divided : Sorting and dressing (the wool) 6, Spinninge and cardinge 40, Weaving 8, Sheremen 6, whereof 2 may be to help the rest. Two stone being 28 lbs. will make 18 yards, yarde broade (i.e., one kersey). One stone spinninge 2s. 4d., Weavinge a piece 20d., Walkinge (i.e. fulling) 3s. 0d. (error for 3d.), Burleing 2d., Dressinge 10d. And 40 spinners will spinne in the week 20 stone. One gallon cyvill (Seville) oyle will serve to 4 stone white woolle."

The estimate will bear examination. The most important facts to be deduced are (1) there is no provision for dyeing, for kerseys were sold in the white or undyed ; (2) a spinner could only spin half a stone of wool in a week ; (3) ten kerseys could be woven by eight weavers in a week. There is reason to think that this was very near the average output for the small clothier weaving his own cloth appears to have aimed at having one piece ready for the market each week. The report proceeds to comment on the proposal :

" The woolle about Sciptoun will make no carsies except it be very pure white ; and at Hallifax there is no cloth made, but yearde broade carsies. If the stuffe that is to be bought for lyttinge (dyeing) were cheape and easie to be gotten, brode clothe were the best kinde of clothe that is to be made about Sciptoun, bycause it is course woolle. Hallifax men occupie (use) a fyne wolle most owt of Lincolneshire, and there corse wolle they sell to the men of Ratchdeall (Rochdale).

These last remarks are very valuable evidence showing that only the finest Craven wool was suitable for the kersey manufacture, which in the main drew its supplies from Lincolnshire. The coarse wool of the moorland sheep was no longer good enough. They also imply the presence in the district of wool-staplers and dealers who were distributing the wool after sorting to meet the requirements of the different localities.

In the 16th century the middlemen were not called staplers in Yorkshire but rather woolchapmen or wooldrivers. Thus the name of a Wakefield merchant who paid 40d. poll tax was Robert Wulchapman, and in 1580 Wm. Hoole "wooldriver," was living at Sleadhall, Brighouse. They were not popular, for the rise in the price of wool was laid at their door, and the State made an attempt in 1552 to do away with them altogether. In future wool might be bought either by merchants of the staple for export to Calais, or by the clothiers, but by none other. As a matter of fact the larger clothiers even in the West Riding spent a considerable portion of their time travelling to the fairs, such as Ripon, Doncaster, Beverley, perhaps Lee Fair and later Wakefield, and further afield to the farms and fairs in the Midland counties to buy their wool. But to the small clothier, who made a kersey a week this was impossible. He could only buy from hand to mouth ; when he sold a kersey in the market he used the money to buy a stone or two of sorted wool for the next piece.

Therefore the Act of 1552 raised a storm of protest from the small clothiers of the kersey district, both in the West Riding and Lancashire. Halifax took the lead so successfully as to obtain by the Halifax Act of 1555 full permission to retain the wooldriver. Any persons living within the parish might buy wool wherever the clothiers did, provided they carried the "wooles so bought by them to the Towne of Halyfaxe, and there to sell the same to suche poore folkes of that and other parishes adjoyning as shall work the same in(to) clothe or yarne."

The preamble of this Act is famous for its vivid description of the small clothier, neither able to keep a horse to carry "woolles" nor to buy much wool at once ; accustomed to repair to Halifax or to some other town nigh thereunto "and ther to bye upon the woolldryver, some a stone, some two and some three or four accordinge to theyre habilitee, and to carrye the same to their houses, some 3, 4, 5 and 6 myles of, upon their Headdes and Backes," and convert it either into yarn or cloth.

This Act probably met the needs of the clothiers of the Huddersfield district, for there is nothing known of protest here, whilst Rochdale and the northern counties around Kendal obtained similar liberty towards 1590.

Having brought his wool home the clothier proceeded to open it out and spread it on hurdles or "fleyks," where it was beaten with swinginge sticks or rods.[1] This was followed by picking to remove bits of foreign matter. The cleaned wool might then be dyed in a vat or "lead," but there is little evidence of wool dyeing until the 18th century. Then came the oiling, or "strinkling" with oil, and a thorough mixing combined with beating. Butter sometimes took the place of imported oil, for the small clothier or weaver always made use of home substitutes when he could. What dyestuffs or chemicals had to be bought came through the salters or drysalters.

The wool was then ready for carding, the object of which was to tease the wool until it was worked up into a flossy ropelike sliver. The name tells of the time when the prickly heads of a teasel (carduus) were used, but not of the fullers teasel on which the bracts are hooked at their tips. In the 15th century, as in the 18th, a pair of hand-cards consisted of wire brushes, in which sharpened and bent

[1] Easther in his *Dialect of Almondbury and Huddersfield* has recorded and so preserved a knowledge of most of the old names of implements and processes used in the district, and has given a short description of the " Home Manufacture of Cloth " that has often been quoted. The Glossary is now invaluable, because it was gathered during years (1846–76) when the domestic industry was still alive and dialect untouched by education.

iron staples were set in a piece of leather and this mounted on a wooden back with a handle to it. The making of these cards was a subsidiary handicraft along the northern edge of this district, for reasons already explained. One of the earliest references to it is the charge against Samuel Brooke, a cardmaker of Clifton, Brighouse, in 1681, of buying foreign iron wire "for making of wooll cards," contrary to the statute.[1]

The sliver from the carding was ready for the spinner, or the spinster, for women were everywhere employed in spinning the yarn, assisted by their children in carding. It was one of the great advantages of the industry in contemporary opinion that it gave universal employment. Children as soon as they could walk might be set to some useful job—even in the 19th century. One writer, about the time of the Union with Scotland (1603), commending the example of the West Riding to the town of Berwick, gave as one of the advantages derived from the industry :

> " The pore and needy shal be releeved by spynninge, oyeling, dressinge of wooll and other easie laboure belonginge to the trade, which yeildeth employment to the eldest, yongest, strongest and weakest persons." [2]

Though a weaver or small clothier might have his spinning done at home, the clothier as a rule put out his spinning to be done in the cottages. For this reason a spinning wheel is often absent from the inventory of a clothier's goods. The output of yarn was so low that wool had often to be sent far afield as there were not enough spinners in the neighbourhood. The cost of spinning given by Ralph Mathew in 1588 seems quite a fair average figure. In the next century spinners in this district could earn at the most 2s. 8d. a stone, or less than three pence a day. A man from Lockwood, giving evidence in 1638, declared that " the wadges for spinninge is not above one penny a day besides meate."

Probably the primitive distaff was entirely displaced by the spinning wheel in the 16th century. The spinning wheel was not the elegant turned and polished instrument fit for my lady's withdrawing room, that is driven by a treadle and was used for spinning flax. This, the Saxony wheel, twists and winds continuously or at the same time, and with both hands of the spinner free it can spin two threads. The " one-thread " wool-wheel, called in Lancashire the " Jersey " wheel (as used for Jersey or combed wool), was of rougher and larger build, as may be seen in the Tolson Memorial Museum. It was also well called the " big-wheel," and this wheel was turned by hand, so that only one thread could be spun on it. Further, the action was intermittent. By turning the wheel the bobbin or spindle was made to revolve at high speed, giving the twist, whilst the spinner drew out the " roving." Then by revolving the wheel in the opposite direction the thread was wound on to the

[1] 13–14 Charles II., 1672–3.
[2] *Letters relating to the Family of Beaumont of Whitley, Yorks.* (1884). See a document printed at the end of the volume.

bobbin. Hargreaves set his eight spindles upright and devised a mechanism for the drawing, but otherwise the jenny reproduced the action of the wool-wheel and retained its big wheel. So also did the slubbing billy.

There were many things to be done before the warp was loomed and the weft was on the shuttle, ready for the weaving ; and the large chamber or bedroom that constituted the loom-shop was littered with a medley of small accessories, as well as bobbin-winders and the warping-wough fixed to a wall. These and the hand-loom itself may be seen at the Museum, and the loom may still be found here and there in the district and in use as near to Huddersfield as Scapegoat Hill.

After the weaving came the scouring and fulling or milling. Invariably stale urine, under the name of wash or weeting, was used in place of fullers-earth to cleanse the cloth from oil and grease preparatory to milling. Easther describes how the weavers themselves (at a later time) " lecked " the piece with this liquor before carrying it to the mill. But every fulling mill had tanks or barrels for the storage of the liquid, which was collected in the villages until gasworks produced a cheap ammoniacal liquor. The scouring and subsequent washing were carried out by driving stocks which came down in a slanting direction so as not to pound the cloth but to swirl it round. The cloth was then carried back again to be dried and burled at home, and once more taken to the mill to be " milled." Falling stocks (that fell more vertically) were chiefly used for this purpose and the pieces pounded by them in a soapy solution until sufficiently thickened and felted.

The piece was once more taken home to be dried and stretched on the tenters, often unduly stretched, to restore the length lost in the milling. The tenter frames were out of doors, generally in the tenter-croft, or tenter-field, adjoining a clothier's house ; and the name survives in Tenter Hill, Deighton ; Tenter-gate, Paddock ; and Broad Tenter in King Street, Huddersfield, known as such in 1608.

The kersey, undyed and unfinished, was usually sold at this stage, " in the balk," either at Almondbury, or in the 18th century at the Tuesday market at Huddersfield, where it was exposed on the churchyard wall prior to the erection of the Cloth Hall.

Finishing or dressing the cloth was in earlier times carried out by the fuller or walker, for his name is attached to the chief tools of the craft, as witness " fuller's earth " and the " walker shears," which in the 18th century, when the finishing had become a separate trade,[1] became known as " cropper shears." But from wills and inventories of the 16th and 17th centuries, wherein looms and shears are named together, it is certain that clothiers then practised the whole mystery of weaving and cloth dressing, and dyeing as well on occasion.

---

[1] So also it was the fuller who was prohibited from using wire cards in finishing cloth by the Act 3 Henry VIII. (1512)—" The Walker and Fuller shall not rowe nor werke any Clothe or Webbes with any Cardes."

The two chief processes in finishing were (1) raising the nap by means of teasles mounted on handles, the tool being called a handle ; and (2) shearing the rough nap to obtain a smooth even surface, this being done by a heavy pair of shears with the cloth spread on the shear board.[1] The two processes might be repeated and alternated, and the cloth was then looked over, burled (or perched), mended by fine-drawers and finally brushed and pressed.

Ralph Mathew named " sheares, handles, tassels " for his dressing tools. With these may be compared the implements bequeathed by local clothiers about the same time. It will be noticed that they speak of a " pair of looms " as well as a pair of shears, as we still do of a pair of steps or scissors.

Isabell Wodd of Lepton left " one pare of Walker Shears."

Wm. Brook of Dalton Hall, in 1581 left " two pair of my best looms and two pair of my best Shears to my son Richard."

John Longley of Dalton in 1588 : " I give to Wm. Longley, my son, my Loomes, Sleas (slays), Press and handles and all my instruments to work cloth withall."

In 1594 Wm. Jackson of Kirkheaton fitted up three of his sons in the trade : " To Thomas Jackson my son a pair of Loomes and my second pair of Shears. To Richard Jackson, my third son my Tenter, my worse Prasse and my worse pair of Shears. To George Jackson, my youngest son, my best pair of Shears my better Prasse and my Shearboard." (Evidently George ought to have been named Benjamin.)

These extracts are rather limited in range as they were all supplied by the late Mr. Legh Tolson from his Kirkheaton collections, but they reveal nearly all the tools required for finishing cloth and owned by clothiers who were weaving it.

When the cloth was made the clothier had to find a market for it. Practically for the whole of this period the local market was at Almondbury, for Sir John Ramsden only obtained his grant to hold a market at Huddersfield in 1671. But nothing is known of the nature or magnitude of the sales at Almondbury after the year 1500. It is more likely that the local clothiers did a larger business at the local fairs in the West Riding, such as Lee Fair, which suffered when Wakefield established a cloth market early in the 17th century. Barnsley also had a cloth fair, and petitioned against Wakefield's new market. There is proof of this use of the Yorkshire fairs in the will of a Norland clothier who died in 1541 and left his brother 20s. with the desire that he would be so good to his (the testator's) wife and daughter " as to sell ther cloth in the faires in Yorkshier."

These channels were not sufficient for the larger clothier, who must have relied upon selling most of his output to London merchants, or those of Halifax, Wakefield, Leeds, or York, for export through the port of Hull. Of the large export of undyed kersies through Hull there is abundant evidence, though chance has not yet

[1] See Chap. X. for the finishing processes in more detail. Rowing with wire cards was a supplementary operation that was certainly practised at Huddersfield, Halifax and Leeds at the beginning of the 19th century.

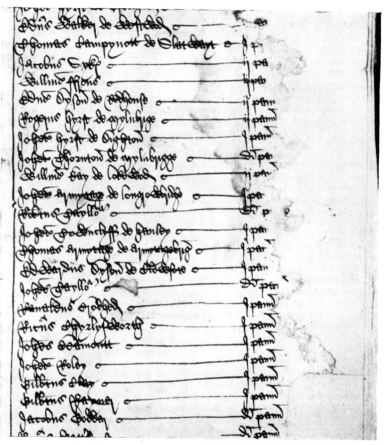

4. ALMONDBURY CLOTHIERS, 1533 (*Facsimile*).
List begins with " Edwd. Walker de Westwod."
Opposite each name is set the number of deceitful cloths, viz :
i., or ii., or a half (de) pann.

revealed any explicit association of Huddersfield with it. To the use
of the London market there are one or two direct references. There
was a great cloth fair held on and about St. Bartholomew's Day, to
which Yorkshire clothiers made a yearly pilgrimage. The booths were
their own property and were frequently bequeathed to their sons.
Thus John Crosseley of Huddersfield, in his will made November 12th,
1562, left " to my eldest sone, Willm Crosley, all my intrest and terme
of yeares whiche I have or ought to have, of and in one standing or
boothe in the clothe faire called great Sainet Bartilmewes, nere west
Smythefield, of London." Some few years later the Almondbury
Registers note the death of another clothier on his way to the fair :

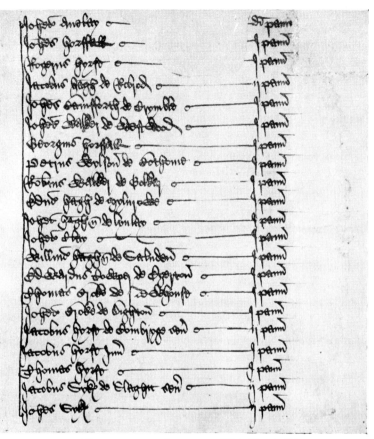

5. HUDDERSFIELD CLOTHIERS 1533 (*Facsimile*).
List begins with "Johes Anelay" and ends with the last name
"Johes Sykes.

"Sept. 1587. Thomas Croslande on journey to London to St. Bartholomew's Fair died unadministered, and was buried at Rodehaye, 2nd September."

Equally famous was the weekly cloth market at Blackwell Hall, where Yorkshire kersies were sold in the " Northern Hall." It was clearly impossible for a Yorkshire clothier to attend this regularly himself, so that it became the custom to arrange for an agent or factor to act for him. It also became necessary to entrust the pieces to pack-horse carriers for conveyance to London, so that a regular system of transport by such grew up towards the end of the 16th century, if not earlier.

Wills and inventories often reveal a man's trade when nothing else does, but good fortune combined with patient searching at the Public Record Office put into the hands of Mr. John Lister many years ago what amounts to a Directory of the Clothiers of the West Riding in the reign of Henry VIII. So it is possible to present here a list of more than a hundred clothiers in Almondbury, Huddersfield and Kirkheaton parishes only half a century later than the Ulnage Rolls which first bring the cloth market at Almondbury into the light. The list not only reveals the expansion of the trade ; it identifies the clothiers engaged in it and attending the market.

It is really a black list of the " Names of those who make woollen cloths with woof called ' flock,' " as Mr. Lister renders the title. The King had appointed a commission, composed of Sir Marmaduke Constable, Sir John Nevyll of Liversedge and John Pullayn, to make an enquiry about the deceitful cloth-making of Yorkshire, and this list, as the result, was handed to Cromwell, Henry's ruthless minister. Thomas Cromwell was in the habit of jotting down such terrible " remembrances " as " Item, to know the king's pleasure touching Master More " ; and " Item, when Master Fisher shall go to his execution, and the other." Earlier than these comes the entry in 1533 : " Item, to remember such as have caused cloths to be flocked in the North, and to know the King's pleasure." What this was is not recorded, but the offence seems trivial enough, as most of the clothiers had only one or even half a deceitful cloth in their possession. At any rate the list is a long one. Halifax parish headed it with 182 names, Heptonstall came second with 60, and there followed Almondbury 55, Leeds 49, Elland 49, Huddersfield 40, Bradford 24, Kirkheaton 18, down to Mirfield 8.

The lists of names of these clothiers under Almondbury, Huddersfield and Kirkheaton are given below in full. They constitute the first directory of the cloth manufacturers of this district ; if not complete, they are certainly representative, for these thrifty northerners had the habit of using up the waste wool as it accumulated, however heinous the practice appeared in the eyes of the law.

The surnames are typical of the district, and the common ones— Hirst, Brooke, Haigh, Dyson, Sykes—are equally common in the directories of a century ago and to-day. The unusual names, Frons, Campynott of Slaithwaite, and Thewles of Thewyus, ring true, and are found again in other contemporary lists. The place names affixed to distinguish a person from his namesake add to the value of the list, though more knowledge of the families of the district is required to identify some of them.

Place names around Milnsbridge and Longwood form quite a considerable group that includes Millrow, Botham Hall and Botham, and perhaps Bankhouse. Longrowbryge (twice) may be the same as Longrod, i.e., Longroyd Bridge. But if it can be identified as a Farnley name, then " John Armytage of Longrowbryge " becomes the same person as John Armitage of Farnley Tyas, the founder of the Kirklees family. Grenehouse is probably Hillhouse near Fartown Green, and Grenhede is the house close to Dalton Green. The Brookes of Bradley were an important family much engaged in trade at this time, with Thomas Broke of Newhouse at their head, and others at Deighton, at Bradley-gate and at the Gate-house.

NAMES OF THOSE WHO MADE WOOLLEN CLOTHS WITH WOOFE CALLED " FLOCKS." [1] 1533.

ALMONDBURY

John Clay of Almondbury
Robert Hyrst of Bankhouse
John Armytage of
    Longrowbryge
Richard More of Owtlayn
John Hyrst of Grenhed
Edward Walker of Westwod
Thomas Campynott of Slatwayt
James Sykes
Williams ffrons
Edward Dyson of Red (Rod ?)
    house
Roger Hyrst of Mylnbrige
John Hyrst of Digton
John Thornton of Mylnbrigge
William Kay of Lokewod
John Armytage of
    Longrowbridge
Robert Tayllour
John Townclyff of Honley
Thomas Armytage of
    Armytagebrige
Edward Dyson of Clowfote'
John Tayllor
Ralph (Ranald) Brodhed
Richard Chyrlysworth
John Beamontt
John Roley
Gilbert Clay
Gilbert Rayner

James Goddar
Richard Watterhouse
Thomas Ramysden
Gilbert ffoxe
William Anley
Thomas Walkar
John Tayllor
Humfrey Cordyngley
Thomas Jowatt
William Lylle
John Shotelsworth
John Roper
John Crowder
George ffyrth
John ffyrth
Thomas Langfeld of Almondbury
George Langfeld
Edward Hyrst
Gilbert Crosley
James Crowder
Laurence Kay of Almbrige [3]
Adam Tynker of Almonbury
Richard Hopkynson of
    Longrodbrigge
Edward Hamson
John Lokewode of Castylhyll
Thomas Hepworth
George Hanson of Lokewode
William Hanson
Edward Dyson of Clowfote Jun

[1] Public Record Office, Exchequer Accounts, bundle 345, No. 25.
[2] Cloughfoot.
[3] Probably in error for Almbrye.

HODERSFELD

John Hyrst of Hodersfeld [1]
Brian Sykes
James ffylles
Roger Kay
Christopher Horsfall
Thomas Blakburn
Roger Borke (? Broke)
John Blakburn
Edward Blakburn
Edward Hamson
Roger Wylkynson
Thomas Burnley of
    Longrodbrige
William Broke of Bradley Yate
Thomas Broke of Yatehouse
Edward Broke of Grenehouse
Thomas Hanson of Bankhouse
George Dyson of Bothamhaull
James Hyrst
Robert Anelay
John Anelay

John Horsfall
Roger Hyrst
James Hagh of Robrod
John Bamfforth of Crymble
John Walker of Westwood
George Horsfall
Peter Wylson of Bothome
Robert Walker of Golkar
Edward Hagh of Mylnrowe
John Hagh late of Honley
John Clay
William Hagh late of Salnden'
Edward Cowper of Egerton
Thomas Broke of Newhouse
John Broke of Dighton
James Hyrst of Combryge sen [3]
James Hyrst Junr
Thomas Hyrst
James Sykes of Slaghu' senr
John Sykes

HETON (KIRKHEATON)

Roger Thewles of Heton
George Thewles
William Hepworth
Richard Broke of Lees (Dalton
    Lees)
John Wood of Lepton
Thomas Wood
Edward Thewles of Thwyus
Edward Hyrst of Dalton Grene
Roger Hyrst
Ralph Senyer of mylne

John Hepworth of Rothorp
    (Rawthorpe)
John Dyson
James Dyson
John Broke of Dalton lee
Robert Swallow of Swallowmyln
James Hepworth of Tybner end
Henry Hepworth of Heton
    Haull
John Hepworth

[1] Probably John Hirst of Greenhead, Huddersfield, who died 1581.
[2] Salendine.
[3] "Cowme Bridge," named in a Kirkheaton will in 1545, appears to be
the same as Fenay Bridge, Cowmes being near at hand.

CHAPTER V.

THE NEW LANDED GENTRY AND THE FULLING MILLS.

The dissolution of the monasteries, 1536–39, had a profound effect upon the woollen industry, stimulating its expansion in Elizabethan days by the social and economic changes that arose from it. The confiscated lands were hastily sold and then resold by syndicates of speculators to smaller men, with the consequence that a new landed gentry arose out of the yeoman class, or from the ranks of merchants. Although new names begin to appear in local history it by no means follows that they are alien to the district. The barren hill-country of the Pennines had few attractions for a southerner. But a prosperous clothier, already settled on a small estate, had every reason to look favourably on the purchase of more land in his neighbourhood when opportunity offered. There was little else in which to invest his profits, unless he lent money to his neighbours on mortgage of their property, for his business did not require much capital. Even more attractive than land was water-power, and an estate that possessed the manorial rights of a fulling mill, or a stream that would furnish water-power, was wholly desirable.

The first local illustration may be taken from the history of the Kayes of Woodsome Hall. When Arthur Kay inherited the small manors of Farnley Tyas and Slaithwaite on the death of his cousin in 1506, he was but a child and the manor house of Woodsome was a medieval timber-built structure, surrounded by a moat. During the half-century that he lived there Arthur did little to alter the character of the house beyond building the chimney in the hall, which remains his chief memorial with its bold inscription—

ARTHUR KAY BIATRYX KAY.

But he greatly improved his estate and added largely to it. Notably he bought the house and manor of Denby Grange, that had belonged to Byland Abbey ; and he developed his Slaithwaite manor by the purchase of Lingards, by the erection of a new manor house on a fresh site, and by building two fulling mills at Slaithwaite and Lingards, or " both the walk mylns at Slaghtwaite," as his son expresses it.

This son, John Kay (1530–1594), was no less enterprising in the improvement of his inheritance. He applied the methods of " good husbandry," bringing Farnley Moor under the plough and dividing it amongst his tenants, stubbing up woodland, planting quickset hedges, marling and liming his fields. He bought Burton mill and both the corn mill and " walke mylne " in Honley. In partnership with John Baylie he bought the manor of Honley with all the woods in Honley and Netherton. The following year, 1573, the two partners built an " iron smithy " (" Honley Smethies "), evidently intending to smelt iron with charcoal supplied from the woods. It was a characteristic adventure of the time, but nothing is known of its duration or success. When he came to retire to Slaithwaite Hall in 1587 he turned over the two fulling mills on the Colne to his son Robert at a rent of ten pounds a year, and sold him the " mylne boke " for eight pounds. The turnover of these little mills a century later will be detailed presently.[1]

Another example is recorded in Morehouse's *Kirkburton*. The manor of Thurstonland with the land and a grange belonging to Roche Abbey was purchased in 1540 by John Storthes of Storths Hall. In the next year he sold off 120 acres or more, with the manor house, to John Walker of Thurstonland, clothier, who had previously leased some of it from the abbey. But as the lord of the manor already possessed an ancient fulling mill at Mytham Bridge, John Walker was debarred from erecting any new mill. His cloth was to be taken to the lord's mill.

The outstanding figure in the district as regards dealings in land was William Ramsden, who by marrying Johanna, the daughter of John Wodde of Longley Hall, succeeded to his Almondbury estates. William Ramsden trafficked in the properties of the dissolved monasteries to such an extent that it was forbidden to sell him any more. He was of an Elland family, and his father, Robert Ramsden or Romsden, had in 1525 received Crawstone or Crowstone Hall in Greetland from his uncles, Gilbert of Sykehouse and Jeffrey of Stainland. William sold it in 1551, though it remained in the family.

Now in the lists of Yorkshire clothiers guilty of using flocks in their cloths in 1533 no less than six Romsdens are named under Elland. Gilbert of Sykehouse and Geoffray are the two brothers just named ; James and Ranold are with equal certainty the sons of Gilbert. The other names are William of Skottes and Robert Romsden. The identity of William remains doubtful, because Skottes appears unknown ; but Robert can be none other than Robert of Crowstone, for he was the only one of that name. So the whole family stands revealed as yeoman clothiers ; and William Ramsden of Longley becomes an illustration of the rise of the new landed gentry out of the ranks of the yeoman clothier.

William Ramsden was succeeded at Longley Hall by his brother John, but before his death in 1580 he had, as " farmer " of the Queen's mills, according to the Almondbury Survey of 1584, rebuilt the fulling mill " annexed to the corn-mill."

In Dalton there were at least three fulling mills on the small Fenay Beck, near its confluence with the Colne. They changed hands several times between 1560 and 1600, but before 1630 Sir John Ramsden owned them all. However, the Kilner family, who were fulling millers, bought one, probably the lowest at Lees, in 1560, and Thomas Kilner certainly leased one of the others as well. When he began to enlarge or rebuild this latter, which may have been the Lower Mill near Briggate bridge, trouble arose between him and John Ramsden who owned the Upper Mill, because his new dam checked the flow of water from the tail-goit of the Upper Mill. The dispute

---

[1] John Kay in 1582 commenced a volume in which he recorded the activities of himself and his father for the benefit of the heirs of Woodsome, and it was continued by his son and grandson. It is now only known through a transcript that was one of the Hunter MSS., and is now in the library of the Yorks. Arch. Soc. (MS. 178). It has been drawn upon by Huddersfield historians, but it contains material of value to the social and economic historian that still awaits publication.

was amicably settled in 1589 when " John Ramsden of Longley, the elder, gentleman," with his sons William and John, consented to " Thomas Kylner of Dalton, the elder," and his two sons " enjoying the dam of one fulling mill newly erected by them and the water course " at a rent charge of 23s. 4d. John Ledgeard of Mirfield and three others were appointed " to set marks on the bridge next above the dam and to ensure that the water from the fulling mill of John Ramsden standing next above be not stopped and that all obstructions be removed."

The story of the Armytage family of Kirklees furnishes the most illuminating local example of the rise of the titled gentry out of the ranks of the clothiers in the 16th century. It is similar in many respects, but the facts are more certain and have never been related. The " site of the late Priory of Kyrkeleys " and the lands attached to it had changed hands several times before they were all bought by " John Armytage of Farnley-tias, yeoman," in 1565. The first point of interest is that John Armytage of Farnley Tyas was a clothier. He was so described in several deeds still in the muniment room at Kirklees, both before and after his purchase of the estate. In 1557 he was " of Farnley, co. York, clothier " ; and in 1566 " John Armytage of Kyrckelies, clothier," leased lands in Huddersfield to " John Horsfall of Huddrysfyld, clothier." In 1541 William Ramsden of Longley had brought a suit against him to compel him to use the King's Mill in Huddersfield for fulling his cloth. In the light of this and of what follows it looks as if one of the attractions of the Kirklees estate to its new owner was that it provided ample water power for a fulling mill on the Calder.

By an extraordinary chance the trading adventures and death of John Armytage are recorded with much circumstantial detail in the Town Books of Liverpool, now in course of publication. It was then the custom to make a " town bargain " with traders who came to Liverpool, for the purchase of their cargoes of fish or corn, and to share the produce amongst the participants in the deal at a price arranged by the mayor. So the garrulous Recorder of Liverpool relates how " John Armetage of Farnelaye Tyes " came in the spring of 1563 with his partner William Owthwayte of Denmark in the ship " Jesus of Hull " laden with Danish rye, and how he would neither make a town bargain, as he could not get his price, nor pay for a licence to sell in the open market. He therefore tried elsewhere, but the venture proved disastrous in spite of attempts to sell the rye at Warrington, Preston, Carnarvon and other places, and the aid of the courts was sought both by and against Armytage, so that there are echoes of the dispute until the end of 1565.[1]

Once again, about February, 1573–4, the Recorder takes up his pen to tell of the death of Armytage, shipwrecked off the Irish coast and murdered by Irish rebel troops. His story, in modernised spelling, runs thus :—

To register the loss of the boat the Swan of Liverpole, Wyn-

[1] *Liverpool Town Books*, edited by J. A. Twemlow, Vol. I., pp. 201–208.

stanleys owners, Edmund Laurence of Liverpole master under God, the good marchaunt master John Armetaige of Farneley Tyes in the county of York, alias clothier, with his rich stock from Liverpole to Knockfargus (i.e., Carrickfergus), (and) an other courteous gentleman, . . . Hughes of . . ., after ship wreck came to land and fell amongst the rebel Kernes, and were there most villainously murdered, slain and cut in pieces as the vilest kind of flesh, contrary to the pleasure and will of God . . .[1]

Rightly, Armytage is described as merchant or clothier, for he was both, and there can be very little doubt that this time the rich stock on board came from the looms of Almondbury and Farnley Tyas. Absolute confirmation of the narrative and the identity of John Armytage is forthcoming in the subsequent valuation (still preserved at Kirklees) of the estate of " John Armytage, gentleman, who died 21st February 16 Eliz." (1573–4). His ambitions are shown also in another direction, for in 1564 he sent his son, John Armytage the second, to Trinity College, Cambridge, and in 1566 entered him at the Middle Temple to become a barrister ; and this son married the daughter of a Hull merchant. The third John Armytage followed in the steps of his father and became High Sheriff of Yorkshire in 1615. The baronetcy came in the next generation, and the descendants of John Armytage have lived at Kirklees down to the present day.

Nothing is heard of the fulling mill on the Calder until 1579, when the son, John Armytage the second, acquired " a parcel of land and water in Rastricke called Oldfirth for . . . a pool for a fulling mill built there," but with a reservation for " sufficient way for all carts . . . through and across the water." This Oldfirth was the old ford across the Calder immediately below the bridge that now carries the Huddersfield road into Brighouse. The fulling mill existed there in 1555, and probably in 1494, so that what John Armytage planned was a new dam to obtain a greater head of water for his mill, that was afterwards known as " Lower Mill."

A little higher up the Calder was the ancient manorial corn mill of Rastrick, or Brighouse, near the old bridge. This had been leased in 1478 for a term of forty years with permission to add to it a fulling mill, though one does not appear to have been built until 1518 or 1519. Ten years after John Armytage had planned his improvements at the Lower Mill, the owners of the Upper Mill laid a complaint that his dam had been built right across the river instead of half-way and had been raised two or three feet, by him or his under tenants, so that the Oldford was generally under water and the Upper Mill was being flooded at " every small flood." [2]

The result of the lawsuit is not known, but the point of interest is that the Armytages, father and son, acquired a fulling mill and that its enlargement caused the usual conflict with neighbouring owners. Both fulling mills continued in use into the 19th century.

But it is the Brooke family (of John Brooke & Sons of Armitage Bridge) which provides the most perfect link with the fulling mills of

[1] *Ibid.*, Vol. II., pp. 147–8.
[2] *Yorkshire Deeds* (Y.A.S.), Vol. V.

the 16th century. The researches into his ancestry made by the late Sir Thomas Brooke, Bart., reveal an unbroken line of clothiers and fulling millers from the early 16th century. For fifteen generations and through four centuries the family has now been making cloth and has owned or occupied a mill on the waters of Holme. Under its present title the firm has been directed by successive generations for a century and a half. It is an unparalleled record in the industry.

The first, Roger Brooke of Holme, is little more than a name, but his son John by 1541 was leasing the New-mill in Holme[1] and Cartworth Mill a year or two later. The third Roger in Elizabethan days is more definitely " of Greenhill Bank in Wooldale in Holme," and there the family rooted themselves for two centuries. He and his son Humphrey held the Milneholme, the other side the water in Fulstone, and likely enough they occupied an adjacent mill. Two generations later the first William (1636–83) acquired what appears to be the mill at Greenhill Bank, and it may be the New-mill of 1541. The record in the court rolls of the Manor of Wakefield is as follows :—

Court held at Burton, 5 October 33 Chas. II. (1681).

John Rowley of Butterly on 3rd October inst granted to the use of William Brooke "All that New Milne water in a certain place called Millwood, with mill, house, fullery pool and pond then built . . . and to convey the same water called New Milne Water in through and beyond the said premises."

From these examples it becomes clear that the new Tudor landowners, usually of local yeoman or clothier stock, encouraged the growth of the industry by the provision of more fulling mills. The total number was not large ; probably only the Ramsdens of Longley and the Kayes of Woodsome owned more than a single mill. Nor does the number appear to have risen apprciably under the Stuarts. An agreement quoted by Morehouse and considered below implies that early in the 18th century there were only seventeen at work on the Colne and its tributaries. Some of them had grown out of the manorial corn-mill and all were manorial in origin. Tenants of the manor owed suit to both alike. This is shown by an agreement made by Sir John Kaye in 1688, in which the tenant's obligations were stated to be : " to make suite to the corn mill and fulling mills in Lingarths and Slaughwaite with all his corne and cloathes there to be ground and fulled and pay his part for the premises toward repairing the Dams belonging the said severall mills."

Usually a fulling mill was let to a miller who " farmed " it, paying a fixed rent and making his own profit. Thus, in 1594 the fulling mill at Honley (with the miller's cottage) was let at 16s. 8d., with which may be compared the rent of the corn-mill and house, £6 13s. 4d. In this year, when John Kay died, " the fulling mylnes at Slaghtwait " were not rented out of the family. This happened again, nearly a century later, and in consequence the Rental Book of the Dartmouth estate contains over a period of years, 1678–1688,

[1] This gave its name to the hamlet " New Mill," a mile and a half east of Holmfirth. It was a second manorial corn mill, dating at least from the 14th century.

details of the receipts and outgoings of the mills in the charge of
millers paid by piece rate. By that time there was some competition
for the custom of clothiers who lived beyond the confines of the
manor, for these " strangers " could have their cloths milled at a
lower figure than the price fixed for tenants of the manor. This much
is evident from the first detailed entry, though the practice was
scarcely formulated or reduced to rule that year. The whole entry
reads :

"1678. The two Fulling Milns milned this half yeare 1740 peices
which att 6d. a peice comes to £43 10s. 0d., butt strangers for their
encouragement hath usually something returned. The Milner's
wages this half-yeare came to £8 5s. 11d. Other disbursements about
the Milns for this half yeare came to £28 8s. 4d. of which £23 of itt
was for a new house at the lower miln and a new wheel making so
that the remainder of this half yeare came butt to £6 15s. 9d."

This modest trading account of the fulling mills, except for the
heavy renewals, is representative. It will be noticed that it only
covers half a year, for as the mills only ran through the winter and
spring to avoid the drought of summer, they were only accounted for
at the " Whytsontyde Rentall." The combined effect of winter frost
and summer drought is shown in the Rental of 1684 when the receipts
fell to the minimum of the decade. It also gives further details of
considerable value.

"1684. The two Fulling Milns milned this half yeare (notwithstanding the long and great want of water thorow the longest Frost
and Droughtyest summer that was ever heard of) 1435 peices, 271 of
them was Strangers out of the Mannor or Lordshipp of Slaighwaite
and these payes but 5d. a peice if they have six or above upon
account. The remainder are 1164 which are all made within the
Lordshipp and these pay 6d. for every peice. The Milners wages
(they have 5 farthings for every peice milning) amounts this halfe
yeare to £7 13s. 7d. with 12d. given to each of them and other disbursements about the Milns and Damms to £4 6s. 4d., soe that this
halfe yeare cleare profitt if all be gott will amount to att the rates
abovesaid £22 15s."

This half-year's trading account is so complete that it may be
set out in modern form :—

SLAITHWAITE FULLING MILLS.

Half Year ending Whitsuntide 1684.

RECEIPTS.	£	s.	d.	PAYMENTS.	£	s.	d.
By 1164 kerseys fulled				To Milner's wages for			
@ 6d. ...	29	2	0	1435 kerseys @			
271 kerseys fulled				1¼d.	7	9	7
@ 5d. ...	5	12	11	Bonus, 4 men @ 12d.	0	4	0
				Repairs and renewals	4	6	4
1435				Trading profit ...	22	15	0
	£34	14	11		£34	14	11

Truly, the scale of business was not large in those days, but population was still very thin and scattered in the upper parts of Colne Valley. In the good years the two mills fulled about 1,800 cloths, of which 300 or more were brought by strangers, so that the weekly output was 50 or 60 cloths. Perhaps it is a generous estimate to imagine some 50 clothiers in Slaithwaite bringing a kersey a week to one mill or the other for thirty weeks between October and Whitsuntide, and some ten clothiers from beyond the township contributing the balance at the same rate. Then from hay-time to harvest, weaving gave place to farming, and clothiers and millers alike were working on the land when weather permitted.

The milners' wages took from £7 10s. 0d. to £9 10s. 0d. in the half-year, and with two mills there were two milners. The gratuity or bonus of 4s. implies four recipients, and the other two would be boys or apprentices, otherwise unpaid. So the weekly wage of each milner might be, but could hardly exceed three shillings, and out of this he had to provide materials, particularly soap, as was the custom long afterwards. But he had his house free, and he probably received tips from customers for each cloth that he fulled for them.

The lord's " cleare profitt " nearly touched £30 in 1679, when the allowance to strangers was fixed at a penny a cloth, and only fell below £23 in a second lean year, 1685, when " because of the badness of trade thorow Munmouth's rebellion " only 1,568 pieces were milned.

Further light upon the question of competition for custom is shown by an interesting Agreement that is given in full in Morehouse's *Kirkburton*. It was entered into by the " Owners and Farmers of divers Fulling Mills, in the parishes of Kirkburton, Almondbury, Huddersfield and Kirkheaton," and dated 7th October, 6 Anne, 1707.

There were seventeen seals but only thirteen signatories to the agreement, which set out that the " Owners and Farmers " (1) would not " full or milne any manner of Cloth in or by any of their respective Mills on the Sunday or Lord's Day . . . at any time during the space of seven yeares " ; (2) would not deliver the cloth to the owners until they had been paid for the fulling ; and (3) would not charge less than sixpence for every piece of Cloth under eighteen yards, eightpence for pieces between eighteen and thirty yards, and twelve pence if over thirty yards. The other party to the agreement was William Bradley of Huddersfield, Salter, who was to act for the Owners and enforce the penalties, and whose name survives in Bradley Mills.

The document is valuable as revealing joint and voluntary action by the fullers both in fixing minimum prices and abolishing Sunday labour. Heaton quotes an order of Quarter Sessions prohibiting the the " common practice to mill Narrow Cloth upon Sundays " which had increased to a " Scandalous and Shocking Degree," but this was thirty years later. Possibly the Huddersfield fullers failed at the start to secure unanimity ; at least the four missing signatures suggest it, and it is not likely that the attempt to prevent cut prices was successful for long.

The last document to be noticed, almost contemporary with the preceding one, suggests that the Slaighthwaite mills were no longer to enjoy a monopoly of the trade of the upper Colne valley. It shows the inhabitants or clothiers of Marsden taking practical steps to encourage a miller to set up a fulling mill in their township in 1709. It recites :

" That whereas the hamlet and Mannor of Marsden . . . is destitute of a fulling Mill and that it would be a publick convenience and advantage to the Inhabitants thereof to have a fulling Mill within the said Mannor and whereas there are some proposalls made by Robert France of Edgend . . . for erecting and setting up a fulling Mill within the said Mannor.

" Now for his encouragement therein We whose names are hereunto subscribed do . . . promise . . . that the said fulling Mill shall be . . . freed . . . from all manner of Layes Taxes and parochial inquisitions whatsoever excepting only the rents and services that shall be due to the chief Lord . . . of the Mannor."

To this there are forty-two names appended, with John Marsden of Pule at the head of the list.[1]

CHAPTER VI.

THE CLOTHIER'S HOME.

The clothier and the fulling miller were the two pivotal figures in the industry, and their habitations were the centres at which the respective stages of the manufacture were carried out. Their location was quite distinct, for the clothiers lived and worked on the hills. Almondbury, Highburton, Honley, Meltham, Oldfield and Thurstonland all lay high up and could only be approached by a steep climb, a " bank," from the valley ; but their old fulling mills were in the bottom.

The fulling mill and its bridge became in later centuries the nucleus of modern industrial villages, and this growth has wholly altered the appearance of the valleys. Hardly an ancient mill, even of the 18th century, survives in the main valleys ; but in more secluded ones, such as Merrydale or Deanhead, crumbling isolated mills with perchance a narrow stone bridge and a dam-site or a wheel-house, though later in date, serve to show the typical setting of an old fulling mill. Perhaps the best illustration is the old corn-mill at Thunderbridge that served Shelley and Shepley, and Woodsome Mill is another that has not lost its rural aspect.

But the clothier's home as it was in the 17th century can still be seen on the uplands, often with additions made in the next century to meet the expansion and larger organisation of his business. There is not the wealth of them that is to be seen in the Halifax parish, but

[1] The Memorandum is given in full in *Ye Chapell of Marsden*, by A. R. Barrett, p. 39.

6. A Clothier's Home and Warehouse at Lumb, in Almondbury.

there are examples enough to show their wide distribution on the uplands, either isolated or in the hamlets, or in what were hamlets.

In varying degree these show certain characteristic features, the most universal of which is the long many-mullioned window of the chamber on the first floor. Two old inns at Slaithwaite have each an upper window of fourteen lights and the " Old Ram " at Marsden (now closed as an inn) has one in the rear of nineteen lights, the whole length of the building. These were undoubtedly all built to serve both as weaving rooms or " shops " and bed chambers.

One of the best illustrations is the secluded homestead known as Lumb in the township of Almondbury, where the Parkin family lived for four centuries near the foot of Castle Hill (Fig. 6). It is complete, for it comprises (1) the house, long and low with a range of long upper windows and a cottage at one end ; (2) on the left, the laithe or farm building composed of barn for the corn and hay, mistal for the cows, stable for a horse or two ; (3) a taller and usually a later building to serve as " warehouse," often with steps outside up to the " takin-in " room or the first floor ; (4) on the right a low building or shed for " lead-house " or dyehouse. The warehouse rather belongs to the 18th century than to the 17th century, for the need of it only arose when the master-clothier began to be a manufacturer, employing cottage labour, providing wool for carding and then yarn for weaving, and receiving the yarn and the pieces again on his premises. Hence the usual name for the warehouse, the " takin-in " place. But it is a characteristic adjunct in the domestic stage of the industry. Here also in some cases, if he finished the cloth, there was room for a number of cloth-dressers working in the warehouse, in the "croppers-shop." To these buildings must also be added a supply of running water, from a spring or well, for scouring and dyeing either wool or cloth ; and one or more tenters in the tenter croft, or tenter-field.

Although the contents of all such yeomen's houses are long dispersed, it is possible to obtain a very real idea of the mode of life within them, by the aid of published inventories of the period and the relics gathered in the Tolson Memorial Museum. Perhaps some day, when the opportunity arises, one of these homesteads will be converted into what would be an ideal folk-museum by refitting it with the furniture and implements of the yeoman-clothier in the 17th or 18th century. Meanwhile a selection from the goods left by a Saddle-worth cloth-maker, Joseph Schofield of Arthurs,[1] who died in 1712, will serve to furnish, as it were, Lumb in Almondbury, or the cottage at Bottoms (Fig. 7).

His farm stock, both live and dead, was to be found mainly in and about the laithe. " One ould cow, a heifer, a sterke and a calfe " were valued at £9 ; " eight young sheep " at £1 10s. 0d., and he had also " in stocks of bees, at home and abroad," £1 10s. 0d. Doubtless some of the hives were at a distance, perhaps amongst the heather. But it was the clothier rather than the farmer who needed " one little horse, pack-saddle, and other gayres (gears) belonging to him "

[1] See Ammon Wrigley's *Songs of a Moorland Parish*, 1912, pp. 19–21.

7. A Weaver's Cottage at Bottoms, in Almondbury.

worth £3 5s. 0d. The farm implements included "four sledges, wheelbarrows, rakes, a harrow, two ladders, pitchforks, a skuttle and two ridles " entered at 13s., with " sythes, sickles " and sundry tools valued at 7s. " In corne and hay " he had £4 and " in Maynour (manure), turves, coles, thatch and some other od huslement " 5s. The only dairy utensil named in the list was a "cheese presse," though the " flesh, cheese and butter " in the house to the value of 13s. would all be home produce.

The following entries cover most of Schofield's textile implements and stock in trade :—

	£	s.	d.
One packe of woll and flocks, together with the workmanship already done at the woll ...	8	2	6
One course piece of cloth, at Hudersfld	1	6	0
One payre of lombs (looms) with healds and slay and all material belonging	1	5	0
Two payre of lombs with lomb stocks, wheeles, cards, wiskitts, baskitts, warpeing walls and creeles	0	10	0
One dyeing lead and a payre of tainters (tenters)	2	5	0
Weigh beam and scales, sacks, woll pokes, one ould packcloth, a mustart ball and some lead weights	0	6	6

Some of the names call for explanation. The " wheeles " would include a spinning wheel and a winding or bobbin wheel. "Warping-walls " is another form of " warping-woof," the use of which is described by Easther (p. 145). The Museum contains an example both of it and the creel. A " whisket " or " wiskit," noted by Easther, was a basket ; but perhaps the name was restricted to a particular form used as a pannier, a pair being slung across the back of a horse, or "mule," i.e., a donkey. The name appears to have died out with the disappearance of pack-horses. A "mustart ball " was the round hand-mill for crushing mustard seed.

Ammon Wrigley's comment upon the list is : "Schofield tossed his wool about into a flossy condition, carded it with little hand-cards, spun it on one spindle, warped it on pegs driven into the warping walls, and then wove his piece in a little hand-loom."

It is also clear that he dyed at least some of his wool, but he had no finishing tools, and therefore sold his cloth in the balk or unfinished state at Huddersfield.

The Saddleworth inventory is that of a small clothier typical of that district ; but nearer Huddersfield the clothiers manufactured on a larger scale and often finished their cloth as well.

With an establishment of this size a master-clothier would have possibly one or two apprentices, living with him and bound for a term of years, usually seven. Morehouse quotes several early agreements from a register of " servants and apprentices " kept by the Hepworths of Shepley Hall. One of them sets out that :—

"John, son of Thomas Roberts of Wooldall, is to serve Luke Firth of Booth-house in Holmfirth, from the 2nd January

1602 for six yeares as an apprentice, during which term he is to
be provided by the said Firth with meat, drink, apparell and
lodging and likewise to give unto his said apprentice every
quarter of a year 4d. of money. The said Luke Firth to instruct
his said apprentice in the mystery or science of cloth-working
and weaving the broad lombes. The said apprentice to serve his
said master one whole yeare after his tearme be expired, having
20s. of money at the beginning of his tearme of one yeare."

In another agreement the apprentice was bound for nine years
and was to be taught " the traid of weaveing, warping, dyeing,
shearing and all other things to the said traid and occupation of
cloth-working belonging."

The relation between master and apprentice is further illus-
trated by a bequest made in 1645 by Wm. North of Dalton in the
parish of Kirkheaton : " To Robert Dawson, my Apprentice, a pair
of Loomes and 2 pair of Cloth Sheares towards furniture for his
trade."

CHAPTER VII.

THE EIGHTEENTH CENTURY TO 1760.

In the life-time of a man born here about the time of the
Revolution of 1688 and living to see George III. ascend the throne in
1760, there was scarcely a change in the organisation of the textile
industry, or in his surroundings, or in his daily life, to herald the
swift succession of inventions and the transformation of both industry
and district that were compassed by a single life time after 1760. But
certainly there was no stagnation. Trade was expanding, the population was growing, and wealth was increasing as the industry
developed on the lines already described. Card-setting, carding and
spinning were the constant employment of the cottager, the children,
the women ; whilst the men wove either for themselves or a clothier
through the winter, but in summer laboured on the land as well.

The most significant memorial of this period is to be found in the
numerous stone stoops still standing where they were set up to direct
the traveller at crossways on the open moors. There are a dozen at
least, most of them dated between 1737 and 1761. The one in Thurstonland, between Honley and Farnley Tyas, will serve as a sample
with its directions and distances to Holmfirth, Huddersfield and
Pennystone, and, as an addition, to Honley. The inscription on the
fourth face :

Jon. Hoyle, Constable
Thos. Bothomley, Surveyor
1738

is equally suggestive and characteristic. The illustration (Fig. 8)
shows another one at the cross roads on Haigh House Hill.

There is no doubt that these scattered guide stones are a lasting
witness of the incessant journeying and traffic necessitated by the
industry. At every stage there was transport of material, either
locally or beyond the district, and most of it was along hill roads that

8. GUIDE STOOP AT HAIGH HOUSE HILL.

are now nearly deserted.

Neither should the other lesson they teach be missed. Each township governed itself and looked after its own highways ; none of them was superior to the others. A constable, a surveyor and an overseer elected annually sufficed for the needs of the largest as well as the smallest community. A guide stone directed to Marsden, or Honley, or Slaithwaite, or Elland, as naturally and perhaps as often as to Huddersfield. It is true that the presence of a parish church added to the importance of a few places, and its new market was beginning to exalt Huddersfield beyond its compeers. But down to 1760 at any rate, there was no town life in the district ; no rows of mean houses, no crowding of population into centres for employment in factories, for there were no factories. The industry was distributed throughout the district, as was the population, without any abnormal concentration at any one point. Yet the foci had come into existence and first slowly and then after 1760 rapidly, population began to cluster round the water-mills that constituted these foci.

That the growth of population had set in before 1760 is clear from the statements in '' Some Account of the Parish of Mirfield,'' written by the Rev. J. Ismay to a friend in Cumberland.[1] It gives a most unusual clerical survey of a parish in 1755 ; its population, industries, agriculture, plants, animals, roads, prices and wages ; though its facts are partly vitiated by a carelessness in the printing of the paper. The vicar distinguished six hamlets, of which Hopton, the one nearest Huddersfield, lies between Kirkheaton and the Calder. '' The dwellings at or about Hopton Hall,'' he wrote, '' are increased in less than forty years from three to eleven, and the inhabitants from seventeen to eighty. . . . There are forty pairs of looms for weaving of white broad cloth in the hamlet only '' (alone).

In Lee Green hamlet on the north of the parish, where there were three public houses, a workhouse and a Moravian Chapel newly established ; '' about two years ago only three families lived on the north side of Lee Green, but now the number amounts to twenty-three and more new buildings are about to be erected.'' These hamlets were both upland ; Easthorp hamlet was down near the river and contained the two corn-and-fulling mills (Ledgard and Low Mill). Of the parish as a whole, with something more than four hundred houses and two thousand people, Ismay wrote that four hundred persons were employed in carding, spinning and preparing wool for the looms ; two hundred in making of cloth and there were one hundred pair of looms for the weaving of broadcloth. Some, perhaps many of these, were wage-earners at very low rates, only 5d. a day for '' clothiers,'' *i.e.*, weavers, whilst men servants for '' husbandry '' were paid 7d. and day labourers 12d. Another useful fact recorded by him was that amongst the crops frequently sown were '' wolds for ye dyers.'' By this he means Weld, Yellow-weed or Dyers'-weed (*Reseda luteola*), and not woad, a blue dyestuff.[2]

[1] *Yorkshire Notes and Queries*, I., pp. 201–211.
[2] Both '' wolds '' and woad were in use at Armitage Bridge Mills about 1850–60.

Hopton, like Mirfield generally, was making broad cloth for the Leeds market ; it was just on the edge of that area. Huddersfield continued to make narrow kerseys, as Defoe states in his *Tour* (1726). " Huthersfield is one of the five towns which carry on that vast cloathing trade by which the wealth and opulence of this part of the country has been raised to what it now is, and there those woollen manufactures are made in such prodigious quantities, which are known by the name of Yorkshire Kersies. . . . At this town there is a market for kersies every Tuesday."

The first sign of factory organisation is to be found in the " workhouse," such as the one just mentioned at Mirfield. When these existed, carding and spinning of wool were the usual employment either of pauper children or of vagrants, and clothiers were ready both to find the wool and to pay for the labour. A statement by Thoresby, the Leeds historian, in this connection appears to be the first use in Yorkshire of the term " scribbling " as the equivalent of, or a stage in, carding. Writing of the House of Correction in Leeds, he remarked in 1715, " Part of it is now employed as a Work-house where poor Boys and Girls are taught to *Scrible*, a new Invention whereby the different colours in the deyed wool are delicately mix'd without any Danger of *Raws*." [1] Whether the mixing of wools was a new idea to Thoresby or not, the name scribbling was not limited to that but came about his time to be applied to the first stage of carding. Morehouse, again the most helpful of local historians, wrote in 1861 of scribbling and carding being jointly carried on in the Holmfirth district before 1750.

> " Until the latter half of the last century, the kind of cloths manufactured here were called ' Leeds Reds,' a coarse class of goods, manufactured in the white, or undyed state, and dyed red in the cloth, slightly finished, and then sold to the Leeds merchants. These goods were manufactured in the old form— scribbled and carded by a single pair of cards—spun by a single thread and woven by the hand shuttle." [2]

The new word (if it really was new) began to displace the older and to be used, in Yorkshire at least, for the whole process of preparing the wool with wire hand cards. So, in Saddleworth the parish registers, from 1736 onwards, record the names of many men who were by occupation " scribblers," but never a carder ; whereas, over the border in Rossendale they were all " carders." [3] Consequently, at the end of the century, Yorkshire was calling the mill which housed the new machinery for carding wool a " scribbling-mill," though elsewhere it was known as a carding mill.

At the same time there was in the northern dialects a verb " tum," " tumming " of exactly the same meaning as " scribbling,"

[1] *Ducatus Leodiensis*, 1715, p. 88.
[2] It is likely that these " Leeds Reds " were broad cloths, as the apprentice to Luke Firth of Holmfirth (p. 55) was to weave on the broad loom.
[3] Newchurch Registers quoted in *The Economic History of Rossendale*, by G. H. Tupling, 1929, p. 181.

and like it, applied to the first stage of carding. This was freely used in the Huddersfield district, as well as the Spen valley and elsewhere in Yorkshire. In particular the cardings produced in the process were called "tummings," and when before the middle of the eighteenth century, one of the hand cards was made larger and fixed to a base or stand and only the upper one held in the hand, the carding "stocks" so produced were generally called "tumming stocks."[1]

CHAPTER VIII.

THE TRANSFORMATION AFTER 1760.

The year 1760 is generally chosen to mark the beginning of the great transformation of England that is known as the Industrial Revolution. The term is not a happy one with its suggestion of lightning action, of antagonism to achieve a desired result and of victor and vanquished. Revolution may be the most convenient word to cover all the social and economic changes wrought by the birth of applied science and by the use of mechanical inventions and power in industrial processes ; but if so it must be stripped of its political implications. The Industrial Revolution was, and is in fact, a process—a process of evolution. Watching its course for a century in a single industry in one locality it is possible to trace the sequence of events that gradually produced a factory system out of the domestic woollen industry, and that continually accelerated the rate of production by the substitution of machinery and power for hand labour. There came in its train all kinds of new social and economic problems, some still unsolved, which it is not the purpose of this little history to discuss. Its only concern is to note the new forces that compelled the transformation of the industry and its reorganisation on fresh lines.

The first point to emphasize is that the transformation was gradual and evolutionary. No one can say when it was complete for it is still in progress. A full century elapsed before hand labour was replaced by power-driven machinery ; and that century was crowded with a succession of mechanical inventions and devices, of ideas that had to be translated into practice, at first crudely by wheelwrights and blacksmiths, and then later by the mechanics, millwrights and engineers that were themselves the products of the revolution. Every new machine contained a new idea but it utilised much of the old mechanism. To take only one example, the shearing frames, that aroused more hostility in this district than any other invention, were simply the old croppers-shears, mounted on a travelling frame, and made to open and shut by a revolving crank exactly in the way that the cropper had operated them by hand. It was an attempt to use power with a minimum of change. In another sphere evolution may be traced in the gradual transformation of the clothier's house and warehouse in an upland village into a weaving

[1] See Easther's *Glossary of Almondbury;* and in the *Huddersfield Examiner* an obituary of James Beardsall, 13 Jan., 1856, and "The Humble Homes of Sixty Years Ago," III. 1929 ; also Peel's *Spen Valley*, p. 230.

mill, or a manufacturing unit ; whilst the fulling mill down in the valley grew first into a scribbling mill and then into a spinning mill. The separation of weaving and spinning persists, even if in a diminishing degree, and it illustrates the historic continuity of the change from domestic manufacture to modern methods.

Further, the transformation was brought about by individual enterprise, and if the great inventions are included, by the persistent application of untaught individuals possessed of mechanical ingenuity or even genius, who laboured with their self-imposed problems often under the most discouraging circumstances and with inadequate means and training. The history of the eighteenth century is, indeed, meaningless unless it is recognised that its triumphs are those of the individual, in all realms of human activity. Freedom had brought an enquiring, adventurous spirit, in marked contrast to the lethargy that still prevailed in corporate life, whether in Church, State, or University.

At first the wool textile industry was purely imitative, drawing its inspiration from the inventions in the cotton industry, and applying them to a less tractible fibre where it could ; but retaining hand methods to a much later date where Lancashire machines were impractible. That the news of these Lancashire inventions, Kay's fly-shuttle, Hargreaves' spinning jenny, Arkwright's scribbling or carding engine and Crompton's mule, filtered into Yorkshire chiefly through Huddersfield and Halifax is certain. These districts lay nearest to the Lancashire border, they had a common interest with the woollen manufacture of Burnley, Colne, Rossendale and Rochdale, and had direct access to south Lancashire by the highways over Stanedge and Blackstone Edge. Saddleworth, though the seat of a domestic woollen industry, was from its situation already sharing in the typical Lancashire manufactures of fustians and linen,[1] so that the new cotton industry rapidly and naturally invaded it and other Yorkshire valleys close to the border.[2] Another reason for anticipating the early introduction of the carding machine into this district, even before Arkwright's patents were revoked in 1785, is to be found in the fact that nearly all the cardmakers, both for wool and cotton, were established within the Calder valley in a very circumscribed area, having Brighouse for its centre. Undoubtedly these men had knowledge of the machines, and were ready to equip or " clothe " them with cards suitable for scribbling wool.

Improved means of communication was one of the first stages in the transformation. There was not only a growing need for easier access between the market towns either side of the Pennines, but between them and the sea ports. Whilst Leeds and Wakefield had their eyes chiefly on Hull, Manchester aimed at reaching both Hull and Liverpool ; and whatever either achieved immediately benefited the whole textile industry throughout south Lancashire and the West

[1] Linen-weavers and Fustian-weavers are often named in the Saddleworth Registers from 1722 onwards.

[2] Keighley, in touch with Colne, was the site of the first cotton spinning mill in Yorkshire.

Riding. It is true that the market towns, and Manchester foremost, all sought to put themselves on the great highways leading to London, but most of their effort throughout the eighteenth century went in turnpiking roads and making navigable waterways to link east coast to west coast and themselves to both.

The very first step was the corporate action of certain men of Leeds and Wakefield to improve the navigation of the Aire and Calder so that the cloth brought to their markets could be carried to Hull by water. It was a significant step because it introduced a novel idea, the combination to provide capital to carry out a public work of utility, and it is noteworthy because this waterway, with later improvements, is still efficient in carrying on the transport for which it was designed. Sir John Kaye of Woodsome, in recognition of his parliamentary services in procuring the Act, was invited to the ceremony of opening the locks in 1700.

9. SIR JOHN RAMSDEN'S CANAL: THE BASIN AT ASPLEY.
John R. Gauld.

The Calder and Hebble Navigation Act of 1758 was the next advance, making the Calder navigable from Wakefield as far as Sowerby Bridge. This canal skirted the Huddersfield area, and it was not long before Sir John Ramsden obtained powers to construct a branch canal from its nearest point at Cooper Bridge into the heart of Huddersfield at the King's Mill. This was opened about 1780 and Huddersfield had then a direct waterway to Goole and Hull. The illustration (Fig. 9) shows the canal basin at Aspley with the warehouse of the Aire and Calder Navigation.

Though the Duke of Bridgewater's canal, commenced in 1759,

was not made to meet the needs of the textile industry, it was the first link in the chain, or rather the net, of canals that linked Lancashire and the West Riding early in the next century. But the difficulties of crossing the watershed were beyond the engineering skill of the eighteenth century. So for a time the historic highways over the Pennines had to serve the needs of Lancashire, and it was Manchester and Rochdale who set about improving them by converting three of them into turnpikes. As early as 1732 Manchester took in hand the turnpiking of the road up Longdendale to Salters-brook on the county boundary, and three years later of another through Oldham to Austerlands. In the same year (1735) Rochdale started to turnpike the Blackstone Edge road, but went further than Manchester by carrying it right into Yorkshire as far as Halifax and Elland. No doubt it received some Yorkshire support, but the undertaking was Rochdale's, and its object is clear—to reach the markets for its cloth, for in a few years the Elland branch was continued into Leeds. As to the Manchester-Austerlands road, twenty years elapsed before powers were obtained, in 1759, to make the Yorkshire continuation of it, over Stanedge and through Huddersfield to Wakefield. This was the first turnpike through Huddersfield and it both opened out Marsden and Saddleworth and gave better access to Wakefield. Ten years later another hill road, Huddersfield and Woodhead, joined up the Salters-brook turnpike and greatly benefited Honley and Holme, whilst a turnpike to Birstall gave a better approach to Leeds. Lastly, the early series of turnpikes was completed in 1777 by the one from Halifax through Huddersfield and Almondbury to Penistone and Sheffield.

Expanding trade and easier transport by carriers' waggons and canal sloop soon brought an increase in population, and it is still an easy matter to note the eighteenth century houses and cottages that sprang up along the line of these older turnpikes. In Almondbury and elsewhere there are rows of weavers' cottages with long mullioned windows (Fig. 10). On the old road to Marsden a number of houses bear the date of their erection, and there are others in the villages. The following will serve as examples :—

J S	J H	R W	S F	I E
1770	1763	1763	1782	1771
Travellers' Rest	Marsden	Slaithwaite	Slaithwaite	Holt Head

Huddersfield itself was now growing rapidly with a rough, uneducated class of industrial workers. John Wesley as early as 1759 wrote of them, "A wilder people I never saw in England." And this working class was won to Nonconformity, for the Established Church was unconscious of the new population and its religious needs. A Baptist community had been founded at Salendine Nook by 1739, and others sprang out of it at Lockwood and Pole Moor in 1790. In Huddersfield, Highfield Chapel was built in 1772 and the Wesleyans started at Old Bank in 1775. Jointly they all bear witness to the beginning of a town population, of an industrial class in the modern sense, divorced from the land.

Huddersfield had in fact become the centre of the woollen

10. WEAVERS' COTTAGES IN ALMONDBURY.

Above—AT BANK TOP.   Below—AT WELL HEAD.

industry for the district around. The building of its Cloth Hall by
Sir John Ramsden in 1766, to replace the open-air market by the
churchyard, set the seal on its pre-eminence and stimulated the
growth of the town. The Cloth Hall was the shrine of the domestic
industry, and yet by the irony of fate it was built when the industry
was welcoming the cotton-born inventions that sealed the doom of
the old system. The shrine flourished for a century, and then endured
as a monument until its brick rotunda was swept away recently as an
encumbrance of the ground.[1]

11. Weavers' Cottages at Ainley Place, Slaithwaite.

Save for Kay's fly-shuttle, the earliest of them all (1733), the
great inventions out of Lancashire related to the preliminary processes of carding and spinning. The fly-shuttle was so simple and
patents so lightly regarded that Kay was unable to prevent its wide-
spread adoption in the scattered homesteads among the hills where
the woollen weavers lived. A witness at the parliamentary enquiry
of 1806 stated that it was introduced into Yorkshire in 1763-64 ; and
it may have been in general use by 1770.

By that time Hargreaves had patented his spinning jenny, of
which there was the more need as the fly-shuttle had speeded up
weaving, which was always ahead of the output of yarn from the
spinning wheel. The jenny required little or no adjustment to serve
the woollen industry and it soon began to displace the one-thread
wheel. Morehouse states that it made its way into the Holmfirth
district about 1776. " It (then) contained about eighteen spindles
and was hailed as a prodigy. They rapidly multiplied in numbers as

[1] Description of the Cloth Hall will be found in Ch. xi,

12. Old Market Place and The George Inn, Huddersfield. *c.* 1800.

well as in spindles." Probably forty may be taken as an average of
the number of spindles for the next half century.

For cotton spinning Arkwright's water-frame or throstle, driven
by power from the start, and a little later Crompton's mule, took the
place of the jenny, which was worked by hand. But to the woollen
industry the jenny was invaluable and was in use everywhere, in the
spinner's cottage and the clothier's house, for half a century. Indeed
the fly-shuttle and the spinning jenny suited the domestic industry
perfectly. Every weaver learned to spin on the jenny, every clothier
(or manufacturer) had one or more in his house, and also kept a
number of women spinning yarn for him in their cottages. So began
the growth of the manufacturer's " warehouse " in the upland
hamlets. With a few hand-looms and jennies on his own premises,
and all the hamlet spinning or weaving for him in their homes, he was
able to take a number of pieces to the Cloth Hall each week. But he
was still purely a domestic manufacturer ; there was no power at his
command, nor any mill or factory in the hamlet.

It is possible to see inside the house of one such small clothier,
Joseph Broadbent of Honley, who died in 1779, just before the
scribbling machine made its appearance. The inventory of his goods
was probably drawn up by his friend and fellow-clothier, John Brooke
of Honley, the founder of the firm of Messrs. John Brooke & Sons,
for the list still lingers amongst the early books and papers that are
preserved by his descendants at Armitage Bridge.

Two living rooms downstairs with a fire-range in each, and two
chambers above and a pantry or milkhouse beyond were the sum of
the accommodation. The " house " proper was furnished with
clothes-press, clock and case, pewter case and dresser and pewter, an
oval table, three chairs and three stools, with a few kitchen utensils.
The parlour, as usual, contained the best bed, a small table, six
chairs with bass bottoms and three oak ones ; the " large bibell "
was on the table and two pictures and a map of America hung on the
wall.

The Great Chamber held a bed and a chest, whilst a good store
of oatmeal to the value of £3 10s. 0d. filled two arks in it. But mainly
it was the carding room, for it contained " 2 card stocks & scripling
stock, and cards, hernes & plats 7s. 6d." also " 2 spinning wheels 5s."
and " weigh balk & scales & lead weghts 5s. 6d."

The Little Chamber was definitely the loom-shop, although there
was a small bed in it. It was not so little for it held

	£	s.	d.
Looms & Gears	1	4	0
A Spinning jinnee	2	10	0
One caske of Oil	7	0	0
Oile cistrian (cistern)	0	15	0
A pair of worsted looms	0	10	6
A pack of wooll	12	8	6
11 pd. of white wooll	0	14	6
1 hundred (weight) of Barwood	1	1	0
½ hundred of Brazell-wood ...	1	3	0

There was no cloth in the house except " 13 yds. of worsted shag 2s. 6d. p. yd." in the parlour, and that is explained by the worsted loom, which is the surprise of the inventory. There remain two other items : the " Tenter 31 yds. £3 15s. 0d." was out of doors ; and " Cloath out at makeing & in markett £43 13s. 0d." reveals a fair stock, some of which was being woven off the premises.

Joseph Broadbent also, like all the clothiers, had his small holding or little farm to furnish food for his family. There were two cows (£12 12s. 0d.) in the mistal, and a " mare galewy " (galloway), not yet valued, in the stable ; hay (£4 4s. 0d.) in the stable chamber and more hay (£4 4s. 0d.) in stack and field ; while " 36 thrave of oat straw " in the barn line up with the oatmeal in the arks.

The particular value of this inventory is that it shows the jenny adopted, the spinning wheel scarcely abandoned and the scribbling stock still indispensable. A few more years and it also was to be thrown on the scrap heap, but the yeoman-clothier survived and carried on for another half century and more.

Manufacturers like Joseph Broadbent were the life-blood of the Cloth Hall. Often a village had a family or even a small clan of such employers of labour, each calling himself a manufacturer and often sharing a stand in the Hall with his relatives. Thus in the village of Holme there were eight manufacturers of the name of Beardsall in the year 1830. One of them, James, the son of Joshua Beardsall, was born in 1764 and lived until 1856. The curate of Woodhead kept a school at Holme to which James Beardsall was sent until he was seven years of age, when his schoolmaster told him : " James, thou must go home now and learn to spin." As his obituary in the *Huddersfield and Holmfirth Examiner* explains,[1] " Wool was then scribbled by the hand upon what were called ' tumming stocks,' and the spinning was all done upon the spinning wheel, one thread at a time." As a young man Beardsall introduced into Holme the first jenny, one with twenty-four spindles.

" He used to relate," the narrative continues, " having gone to Huddersfield market for thirteen weeks successively without selling a piece ; after which he determined to try Lancashire and took two pieces on his back from Holme to Stockport, a distance of about sixteen miles ; but not succeeding there he went on to Manchester. He continued to sell his goods in the ' country,' as it was then called, and extended his journeys to Birmingham and London. He continued his London journeys for forty years, and was in the early period the only clothier in the neighbourhood who made a practice of doing so. From London he went south-wards, where he met with South-Down wool, and was the first person to introduce it into this district. He also introduced into the neighbourhood the first German wool, having good facilities for meeting with it in London. . . . He was amongst the first to introduce (into Holme) the fancy woollen manufacture, which is extensively carried on by his descendants."

[1] January 13, 1856, reprinted a few years ago.

James Beardsall's business career was a long one and covered many developments, but most of them came early on, as he must have started selling in London soon after 1790. It is also evident that from an early date it must have been a family business, perhaps brothers in partnership. Otherwise he could not have been absent from home for long periods as he was. Nor would the local market at Huddersfield be neglected ; the other brothers would see to that.

THE SCRIBBLING MILL.

The other Lancashire invention that played a great part in transforming the woollen industry was the carding machine perfected by Arkwright in 1775. There had been earlier patents taken out for carding on rollers, but they were ineffective until Arkwright devised or utilised the crank and comb motion for doffing the cardings and so made the process a continuous one. The opposition to his patents and their final revocation in 1785 produced a confusion that still remains ; but one definite fact emerges from the obscurity. Machines more or less identical with Arkwright's carder were beginning to be used in Yorkshire, and in Huddersfield before 1780, for scribbling wool. Few, if any, of the earliest scribbling machines were driven by water power. The first were so small that they could be turned by hand, and they were placed somewhere in the house of the clothier. Then a horse was used to turn a gin which drove the machine, but before long the scribbling machine or " engine " was transferred to the fulling mill where it could be harnessed to the shaft of the water wheel that lifted the fulling stocks. There appears to be scarcely any record of these preliminary stages in this district, and they soon passed away. Morehouse, writing of Holmfirth, says : " The first scribbling-engine set up in this district was in Ing Nook Mill, about 1780. It appeared in a rude state, before the invention of the fly-roller,[1] and seemed to tumble the wool off the cards like flocks."

Apparently this " engine " was driven by water power. Certainly a water wheel was in use to turn some machines in or near Huddersfield that were advertised for sale in January 1779, and described as follows :—

"A complete Scribbling-machine, with new Rollers, carrying 46 Pairs of Cards with Iron-geer in good condition ; together with an upright Shaft, Swimming Wheel and Nutt (capable to carry four machines) with the Tumbling Shaft and Nutt. Also a smaller Machine of seven Barrels or Rollers with Cards in good condition. Likewise a Teazing Mill,[2] on a new construction with the Geer thereto belonging, to go by water. Particulars may be had by applying to J. Kenworthy of Huddersfield, the owner."— *Leeds Mercury*, January 26, 1779.

This is the earliest known reference to the use of scribbling machines in the woollen industry, and it is reasonable to suppose that their development to this stage had occupied several years, so that

[1] Known also as the "fancy."
[2] Otherwise the " willy."

the first trial of them may have come very soon after 1775. Their introduction must be attributed to the clothier or " manufacturer," who soon acquired an old fulling mill, or built a new one, in which he could scribble wool for himself and his neighbours.

Much light has recently thrown upon the rise of the scribbling mill, the machinery within it and its function as a new unit in the industry by the documents included in *The Leeds Woollen Industry*, 1780–1820.[1] One quarter of the volume is filled by the diary of a scribbling miller, Joseph Rogerson of Bramley, and this by itself gives an intimate insight into the whole business and the way it fitted into the domestic industry. The same volume quotes a petition of 1786, that was an appeal to the trade in Leeds not to adopt the new scribbling machines. It stated that there were already no less than 170 in use in the district " extending about seventeen miles south-west of Leeds." This implies that the new machine was then much more widely in use in the Huddersfield, Halifax and Spen valley areas than around Leeds, though some clothiers there were trying it as early as 1781. A reply by one of them admitted the main contentions but emphasised the fact that " out of the 170 machines, perhaps 120 or 130 are very small." In other words only forty or fifty were driven by gin or horse power, and Huddersfield had a considerable share of such.

Though it is possible to trace the scribbling mill from about 1780 there is little insight to be gained of the machinery within it for some years, but by 1790 it had taken shape on lines which it retained for many years. In the next decade it won an established place in the industry without dislocating its domestic organisation, and the number of scribbling mills rapidly rose after the turn of the century when the steam engine began to provide additional power without any limit.

Primarily the scribbling mill was a public mill performing a double function for its customers. It first carded the raw wool brought by the small manufacturers of the neighbourhood and slubbed the cardings, returning the material to its owners (or to their jenny spinners) in the form of slubbings wound on to cops. Later the cloth manufactured from this wool was brought back to the same mill to be scoured and fulled in the stocks. If, however, a scribbling mill was started merely to handle the wool of its owner instead of working for the trade, it assumed a new function and produced a very disturbing effect, as will be shown later.

The plant of the scribbling miller consisted of four different machines, of which three were driven by power and the fourth was operated by hand. These were :—

1. The Willy, or Teazer, which was used to open out and clean the raw wool, also to oil it, or to blend different sorts.

2. The Scribbling-machine, or Scribbler.

3. The Carding-engine, or Carder.

These two were almost identical and consisted of cylinders

[1] Thoresby Society, Leeds, 1831 ; edited by W. B. Crump.

revolving against a much larger central one, called the Swift ; all were clothed with cards to tease out the wool and straighten the fibres. But whereas the wool came off the scribbler in the first stage in a continuous sheet, there was a device on the carder by which it was delivered in 4-inch sections which were immediately rolled into cardings about 30 inches long. The children employed in feeding the machines were called " fillers."

4. The Slubbing Billy.

Very little is known of the origin of the billy, but it is obviously derived from the jenny, and like its parent it continued—with rare exceptions—to be worked by hand. The process of spinning was shared between the two machines, in place of the spinning wheel, and yet the two stages were separated. The clothiers retained the control of jenny spinning, but the first stage, the slubbing, settled almost at once in the scribbling mills. Perhaps it was that slubbing demanded more skill than jenny spinning ; possibly also the need for turning out a product that could be handled and transported caused the scribbling millers to go a step further and make slubbings. At any rate spinning remained a poorly paid cottage industry whilst slubbing became the crown of the scribbling mill and slubbers a class of highly-paid craftsmen.

The object of slubbing was to draw out the loose cardings, putting a slight twist on at the same time, so that the product could be wound on to bobbins or cops. The billy had 30 to 50 spindles mounted on a travelling carriage, and after about eight inches of the cardings had been released they were drawn out to seventy inches by pushing the carriage away whilst the spindles were revolved to give the twist. They were then wound on to the spindles as the carriage came back again. So it had the intermittent action of the one-thread spinning wheel and retained its big wheel. Besides the slubber who operated the billy there were two or three children employed in feeding it with cardings ; they were called piecers or pieceners, as they joined the cardings continuously by rubbing the fresh ones on to the end of the old ones.

It is impossible to present a complete survey of the scribbling mills that had sprung into existence by the end of the 18th century. They were then to be found on all the streams of the district, either by conversion of the old corn mills and fulling mills, or by the erection of new mills. Jefferys, in his large scale map of Yorkshire (1771–2), marks fifty-four of the old kind on the Colne and its tribu-taries, and the number of water mills may have been doubled by 1800. One of us has toured the whole district to ascertain the origin and history of all the older mills, and though a number of firms can trace their rise from this period they have, with few exceptions, to rely upon tradition rather than documents for their early history. It is therefore safer to draw mainly upon contemporary records and the facts given by the local historians. These will furnish samples of the new undertakings and show how the scribbling mills were meeting a demand and fitting themselves into the framework of the domestic industry. It is well to bear in mind that many of them were quite small affairs. Even the firms who loom large in the history of the next century only began on a small scale. Conditions were very fluid and there were many changes and not a few bankruptcies. There was much oscillation between wool and cotton, nor is it at all clear to what extent scribbling was being combined with spinning and weaving. It is not unlikely that a good many clothiers in this district did undertake scribbling as well in a small way, so as to be able to hand out the slubbings to their own spinners, much as they had previously supplied them with wool.

Hughes in his *History of Meltham* describes the origin of the village of Meltham Mills and shows how it was entirely an offshoot of the older Meltham due to the erection of scribbling mills in that valley. In 1780, as in the centuries before, this was just a wild, secluded moorland clough with a sparkling beck tumbling down it and then under the great wood of Honley into Magdale. Meltham was out of sight on the hilltop on the one side and a cluster of houses at Thick Hollins on the other. A footpath from Meltham came down to a little bridge and up through the woods and over the moors to Honley, and at the bridge the tumbling waters of the beck turned the wheel of the old manorial mill that ground the corn grown in the township. Hughes tells what happened after 1780. Nathaniel Dyson, of the corn-mill and manor house, added a fulling mill in 1786 ; but before that, " soon after 1780," William Brook built a scribbling mill higher up the stream. This he used for scribbling, carding and slubbing, and another small mill for fulling. Of course the slubbings went up into Meltham to be spun and woven in the cottages there and thereabouts.

William Brook was enterprising and soon became prosperous. He came to live at Thick Hollins, put up still another small "woollen" mill, and when he found the supply of water insufficient he installed a steam engine to pump the water back again to the dam. By 1805 this " fire-pump " was displaced by a reservoir high up the stream, a novelty due to his son, Jonas Brook, who turned over from woollen to cotton, established the cotton thread manufacture at Meltham Mills and founded the firm of Jonas Brook & Bros. Ltd.

The origin of Meltham Mills tells in brief the whole story of the rise of the industrial valley towns. The rest is mere detail, endless repetition of the same theme with variations. Here are some examples. At the head of the Colne Valley, Ottiwells Mills in Marsden are still remembered as one of the storm centres of the Luddite Riots (see Ch. X. and Fig. 20) ; they had then developed into a factory, for Horsfall was finishing cloth there as well as weaving it. But in this earlier period they were only scribbling mills, for when they were put up for sale in 1801 they were described as " Those two Water-Mills known by the name of Ottiwells Mills . . . near the New Bridge in Marsden. One of which is now used as a Fulling-Mill and the other as a Scribbling-Mill, and both are well supplied with water and fifteen feet of fall to each Mill, now in the possession of Luke Campinot & Co." The machinery, apparently supplied by Rochdale machine-makers, could be taken over by the purchaser. The mills were in the market again in a year, through the failure of the tenant or lessee, and were still owned by Luke Campinot.[1]

At the other end of the district Little John Mill in Brighouse, drawing its power from Clifton Beck, was leased in 1786 as a " fulling mill, scribbling and carding mill." When it was again let to a tenant in 1802 it contained six carding engines. By 1828 it had changed to wire drawing. Reference has already been made to the early history of the fulling mill at the Oldford, known as Brighouse Lower Mills. These were sold by Sir George Armytage in 1816, when they were described as " all those powerful and valuable Fulling and Scribbling Mills . . . consisting of three water wheels, . . . seven double falling stocks, three double and one single driver for the purpose of fulling cloth ; also seventy inches of cards for scribbling and carding wool ; also eight blocks for working wire."

The most informative document is the Dartmouth Estate Book which gives particulars of the mills in 1805. Those on the Holme in the Old Mag lordship are also shown on the Enclosure Award map of 1788 and were situated at Banks, Neiley's, Honley (the old corn mill), at Upper and Lower Steps and Delf Brook, near Armitage Bridge. The Estate Book describes the one at Lower Steps as " a large fulling and scribbling mill, with a detached cotton mill and other buildings, altogether forming the appearance of a Manufactory on a large scale." In 1799 William Beaumont was paying a rent of £54 for one portion and Roberts held another, at £35 ; but from 1804 rented the whole at £350 per annum. Neiley's or Crosley Mill was in the occupation of John Brooke, the founder of the famous firm of John Brooke & Sons. As the growth of the firm is bound up with the rise of the factory it will be considered later.

Still within the Mag Lordship towards Netherton were several more scribbling mills as Crosland and Cocking Steps. Lord's mill was known as Wood Bottom mill, and in 1805 was described as a dwelling house with a scribbling and fulling mill. Cocking Steps mill had been built by the Wrigley family in 1760 (as a fulling mill) and was run by them continuously down to 1924, and for the whole period they were engaged in manufacturing kersies, moleskins, liveries and hunting cloths of the West of England type. It affords another example of the early development from a scribbling mill of a manufacturing business that is characteristic of the district.

The Dartmouth Estate Book (1805) also deals with the mills on the Fenay and Burton stream to the east of Almondbury, all of them fulling and scribbling mills, such as " Fenney Mill, a water, fulling and scribbling mill on a weak small stream held by Daniel Brooke at a rack rent. Lord Dartmouth having laid out upwards of £1,300 on it, the tenant was to have a lease for twenty-one years from May 1789, at a rent of £112, which in the present state of Trade is as much as it is worth."

[1] *Leeds Mercury*, January 25, 1800, and February, 1801. Incidentally it is noteworthy that the name of Campinot has already been mentioned in the lists of clothiers in 1533 (p. 41).

Owing to the small water power, steam was introduced here perhaps earlier than elsewhere, and reference will be made to the others when the use of steam power is considered.

Before taking leave of the 18th century it is necessary to glance at two other innovations that were going to have very far reaching effects on the Huddersfield trade in the next century. These were (1) the use of wool of a finer quality and a higher price from the west and south of England, and especially from Spain and Saxony ; and (2) the making of new " fancy " cloths, different from the traditional broad cloths and narrow kerseys of Yorkshire. Of these the most important at first was the kerseymere, which was a twilled cloth and quite distinct from what a Yorkshireman called a " carsey," though its proper name, " cassimere," from Cashmere, sounded much the same to his ear. The brief sketch of James Beardsall's career, given above, shows him to have taken a share in both these changes. But in the main they were developed in the " factories " ; or it would be nearer the mark to say that they necessitated a factory organisation to ensure effective supervision of the spinning and weaving. So much is clear from the evidence given at the Enquiry of 1806, to be detailed presently.

Both innovations also have their place in a very competent review of the Huddersfield industry published in Aikin's *History of the Country round Manchester*, in 1794. It is clearly based upon internal knowledge of the trade as it existed at the end of the 18th century, and it contains the earliest known reference to kerseymeres.

" The trade of Huddersfield comprises a large share of the clothing trade of Yorkshire, particularly the finer articles of it. These consist of broad and narrow cloths ; fancy cloth, as elastics, beaverettes, etc., also honleys and kerseymeres. The qualities run from 10d. to 8/– per yard narrow ; and broads as high as the superfines in the West of England. The finest broads in Yorkshire are made at Saddleworth, the manufacture of which place are included in this district, being all sold at Huddersfield market.

"These goods are made from all sorts of short English wool, from £6 to £35 per pack ; and from Spanish wool. The lowest priced English wool is chiefly short wool sorted from large fleeces of combing wool bought in Licolnshire, Leicester, Notts., and the neighbouring counties. The finest English wool is from small fleeces in Hereford, Shropshire and other western counties ; and also from Kent, Sussex and their neighbourhood.

" The markets for these goods are almost wholly Great Britain and Ireland and America. They are bought up by the merchants of the clothing towns in a state ready for cropping, dressing and finishing, and are then sent to London and the country towns, or exported from Liverpool or Hull. All the branches of the trade here may be considered as in a thriving state, making allowance for the temporary check of the war, which, however, has been less than might be supposed, as appears from the annual accounts of cloth stamped and registered at Pontefract. It is to be considered, too, that kerseymeres and all other goods carried to the market at Huddersfield which are white and quilled are not registered and these sorts are on the increase."

The description of the Saddleworth trade is more statistical but equally valuable :

"The trade of Saddleworth has increased in a very rapid degree. In 1740 there were not more than about 8,640 cloths manufactured here and those of a very coarse kind. In 1791 the number was 35,639 and in 1792 36,637, which at an average were worth £7 each in an unfinished state, as sold at Huddersfield market, nearly double the value of cloths made in 1740. . . . Many of the superfine broads made here vie with those of the West of England."

The magnitude of the industry in Saddleworth may be gauged from the further facts supplied that there were 76 mills " turned by the Tame and the small streams falling into it," and the looms numbered two thousand.

CHAPTER IX.

THE EARLY NINETEENTH CENTURY

(1) STEAM ENGINE.

The nineteenth century soon brought fresh developments, but it will be well first to note, however briefly, the record of the census taken in 1801, for it helps to keep in truer proportions the growth up to that time and to emphasise the rapid expansion of the next half century. Huddersfield, at the opening of the century, had a population of seven thousand and more within its township ; Almondbury about half the number. Wooldale, that included Holmfirth, ranked next with 2,600, and was followed by Honley, Lepton and Slaithwaite. There was growth, and there was an industrial population, but the centres were still isolated unless in the Colne Valley from Huddersfield Bridge to Longroyd and Milnsbridge. The Church had not yet felt any need for expansion. Huddersfield parish with 14,500 people, Almondbury parish with 17,500 were still served by their ancient churches and chapels without additions. Beyond in the hills, Saddleworth chapelry contained 10,000 people ; so that 50,000 people were living, directly or indirectly, upon the woollen industry and with their interests centred upon the Huddersfield Cloth Hall.

The first and greatest novelty in the nineteenth century was the introduction of steam-power to supplement the water-wheel, to drive the scribbling and fulling mills. Coal had been got for more than a century, to heat the pans of the dyehouse and the hot-press of the cloth finisher, and the seams on the valley sides had been worked by day-holes and adits. But the advent of the steam engine made the

13. HUDDERSFIELD FROM WOODHOUSE IN 1795—*John Stanton.*
Red Doles Canal Bridge and Lock in foreground.

presence of local coal seams a decisive factor in the growth of the industry for the next half-century.

Morehouse states that the steam engine was introduced about 1798 ; John Ratcliffe of Saddleworth, giving evidence before the House of Lords in 1800, stated that there was known to him only " one instance of a steam engine and that a small one," so that from 1800 it was beginning to come into use. At the mill at Cocking Steps, belonging to the Wrigley family, one was introduced in 1801 as shown by the entries in a surviving ledger :

(a) 1801—Mr. J. Jubb,[1] Account for Steam Engine, May 20th.

				£	s.	d.
Oil and paint	...	...	...	0	6	6
Wood for beam	...	...	...	7	5	0
Do. for framing	...	...	...	0	19	0

(b) August 8th, 1804. Insured the Mill with M. Morris, Halifax.

				£
Mill Building	...	...	...	300
Steam Engon	...	...	...	200
Machinery	...	...	...	300
Fulling Mill, etc.	...	...	...	100
Stock-in-trade therein		...	...	100
				£1000

Equally authentic is the evidence relating to the firm of John Brooke & Sons before they left Honley. Shortly before his death in 1878 John Brooke of Armitage Bridge House, writing of his early recollections, told a correspondent : " One of the first . . . but not the very first engine in or near Huddersfield, was put up by my father at Honley at the close of the last century. It was made by Fenton & Murray of Leeds, and it has never escaped my memory that their foreman was a Frenchman of the name of T. Debos."[2]

The Dartmouth Estate Book makes it clear that these earliest steam engines were intended merely to supplement the water-power, to prevent stoppage from lack of water during the dry season, so the mills on the small stream from Kirkburton to Fenay were among the first to use them, and the more readily because this is the one tributary of the Colne that cuts its way through the Coal Measures. In 1805 the entries respecting these mills were as follow :

(a) Rowley Mill :—a fulling and scribbling mill worked by a very small stream and by a steam engine—let to the tenants (Ibberson & Co.) for a lease of forty-two years from May, 1794.

[1] John Jubb was a mill-wright and machine-maker at Leeds. He would not supply the engine.
[2] Quoted in a pamphlet, " John Brooke, J.P.," being his obituary reprinted from the *Huddersfield Examiner*, June 15, 1878.

(b) Dogley or Burton Mill :—a large fulling and scribbling mill worked partly by stream and partly by a steam engine. The mill and 3 acres are held for a lease of 42 years from 1797.

(c) Farnley Mill :—a fulling and scribbling mill built by the tenants (Roberts & Co.) in 1794. This mill is chiefly worked by a steam engine as the water is a very poor supply from a few small reservoirs.

(d) Birks Mill :—a large fulling, scribbling and carding mill, worked by a steam engine, built with stone and covered with slate, with a range of buildings containing four dwellings. The lease (to Dobson & Fisher) to last for 31 years from May 1801.

As Rowley, Farnley and Birks mills were all leased at a uniform nominal rent of £5 5s. 0d. per annum, it is evident that the lessees had found most of the capital required to build or rebuild the mills, as is specifically stated for Farnley Mill.

It would appear that steam engines had been installed in two of them by 1794, and there is an interesting commentary in the Estate Book on the new industrial conditions wrought by their advent. Lord Dartmouth's new agents, who undertook the Survey of 1805, saw that the amenities of Woodsome Hall were already being affected, as witness their

" General Memorandums for Farnley, Rowley and Honley :
" Farnley, of which Woodsome forms a part, is however a very compact property, and being hilly (and) interspersed with large woods, the country would be beautiful to the eye if the number of mills and steam engines now about it did not almost continually contaminate those pleasing Features of Picturesque Beauty, Water and Air.
"The old and respectable Mansion thus surrounded by annoyances can no longer be considered as a fit Residence for the Owner of the Property. However, it is these mills and engines combined with the spirit for Trade in the Inhabitants that stamps an increased value on the Estate and therefore it would ill become us to find fault with them."

In the Colne valley there was more abundant water power available, and Lord Dartmouth through his agents encouraged the erection of new water mills in the neighbourhood of Slaithwaite by helping to find the capital. The Estate Book shows that John Varley was the prime mover here, especially in the erection of cotton mills. He appears to have begun in 1787 by building and running a small wood-rasping and grinding mill at Shaw Carr and then to have added a scribbling mill to the old manorial corn mill, and finally to have built a cotton mill on a third site. The Estate Book tells the story of each :

(a) Shaw Carr Wood Mill : was built by John Varley in the year 1787, when the late Lord advanced £250. Tenant to take a lease for 21 years to commence from this time at £20.

(By 1828 it was a cotton mill with three floors and a warehouse. A fall of eighteen feet drove a water wheel of 24 h.p., but as the water only worked the mill for nine months in the year a steam engine of 24 h.p. was installed.)

(b) Slaithwaite Corn Mill, Scribbling Mill, Warehouse, &c. : The present Scribbling Mill was originally a Corn Mill, but John Varley, the present tenant, proposing to build one on a larger scale he erected a capital stone and slated mill at a little distance below the Old Corn Mill, and also erected a Warehouse a little way detached from the north side of the Corn Mill. These Mills were chiefly erected with Lord Dartmouth's money : as his Lordship gave £1,000 besides the Scribbling Mill. For these Mills an Agreement was made for 25 years at the rent of £160 7s. 0d.

(It was still a scribbling and slubbing mill in 1828, when one water wheel sufficed to drive both it and the new corn mill.)

(c) Waterside Mill :—(A fulling mill) Was burnt down three years since. . . . But the spirit of erecting cotton mills being high at the time Varley, Eastwood & Co. proposed to take the bare stone walls as they were at the old rent of £60 per annum provided Lord Dartmouth advanced £600 at 8% and gave £200 worth of timber : which being done they erected a large cotton mill and are to have a lease from May 1803 at the rent of £108.

(d) The New Mill : Messrs. Shaw & Haigh took an Old Fulling Mill and afterwards proposing to build a large Cotton Mill . . . a large . . . Cotton Mill is erected . . . lease for 31 years from May 1803 at £30.

The history of Linfit Mill on the highway from High Burton to Flockton presents some unusual features. The mill was built in 1815 high up on a small tributary of the Beldon brook, and the choice of site seems to have been determined by the accessibility of coal. From the start it depended wholly upon steam power. Coal was obtained from a day-hole driven into the Black Band seam on the hillside, and was brought down into the boiler-house on a tram road. The first lessees, Smith & Hampshire, equipped it with a 21 h.p. engine to drive six (4 ft.) scribbling machines, six (30 inch) carders, six slubbing billies, a teazer and five fulling stocks ; but by 1817 they had come to grief and the machinery was all for sale.[1] Their creditors were Benjamin Carter of Huddersfield, John Armitage of Kirkheaton, and James Sellers of Wyke, who had evidently provided the machinery, for the first was a machine-maker and the other two card-makers.

Then, in the hands of George Hey & Co., it prospered for many years, for it was near to the weaving population of Kirkburton. To scribbling was added spinning, first by hand and then by power. A large dyehouse and cropping and finishing sheds were built, whilst the weaving was done in the cottages around. In 1851–2 a three-storey mill was added to accommodate power looms and later a weaving shed was built. In all about 130 looms were weaving woollens, fancy trouserings and suitings, and even worsted after 1870 ; and yet the whole place has long been in ruins. It was too remote and too near a colliery district.

14. Scribbling Mill, Merrydale, Slaithwaite.

(2) RESERVOIR AND CANAL.

In the tributary valleys amongst the hills the introduction of the steam engine was long postponed by the making of reservoirs near the sources of the streams, so that the water could be conserved and the flow regulated to meet the requirements of the mills lower down. Several reservoirs were constructed in the Colne basin at various times early in the century, as in the Wessenden valley above Marsden and on Lingarths moor. The most ambitious scheme was the one carried out by the Holme Commissioners, who in 1837 made three large reservoirs in as many moorland valleys to supply the mills both above and below Holmfirth. Unfortunately one of them, the Bilberry reservoir, burst its wholly inadequate embankment in 1852, and the flood wrought enormous damage down the valley and caused much loss of life.

March Haigh reservoir high on the moors above Slaithwaite was made as early as 1794 to supply the mills of the upper Colne valley. Cupwith supplied those on the Merrydale stream down to Slaithwaite. Upper Clough House Mill, or Merrydale (Fig. 14), is described in the Dartmouth survey of 1805 as " a small Scribbling Mill nearly adjoining the farm house and occupied by Sarah Horsfall. This was built about 1785 by Richard Horsfall.'' It may be that this little, secluded mill at Merrydale was one of the earliest scribbling mills in the district, but it is now demolished. Horsfall also built the Lower Clough Mill, which was described in 1828 as consisting of both a scribbling mill in three floors, and a warehouse, dyehouse and dressing shop, though the stream only provided power for nine months in the year. This last is particularly noteworthy for it was a complete and self-contained unit, similar to Linfit Mill, though on a very small scale. The reservoir regulating the water supply enabled the scribbling mill to be brought up into the hills and linked with the manufacturer's warehouse.

But a far greater influence than these reservoirs began to operate early in the century and led to a great expansion of the industry in the Colne valley. This was the new Huddersfield canal, which ultimately linked the Aire and Calder system with the Lancashire system, and converted the Colne valley from a blind alley into a corridor between the manufacturing districts of the West Riding and South Lancashire. The canal was opened as far as Marsden as early as 1804 and was carried through to Ashton-under-Lyne by 1811. It is difficult to realise all that its presence meant to the trade of the valley in pre-railway days ; Slaithwaite for example was not even on a main road, and the canal, with docks and wharves in the village, seemed little short of a miracle. A Directory of 1830, in its information under Huddersfield, assists to an understanding of the part it played at that time. Five firms, with agents in Huddersfield, announced " Water Conveyance,'' such as " Fly Boats to and from Manchester daily.'' One of them appears to have been a local firm, and its announcement reads :—

[1] *Leeds Mercury*, May 10, 1817.

" Huddersfield Shipping Co., Engine Bridge. Sloops direct to and from Irongate Wharf, London ; and Fly Boats daily to Saddleworth, Stayley Bridge, Ashton-under-Lyne, Oldham, Stockport and Manchester, whence goods are forwarded to Liverpool, Chester . . . and to all parts of the South of England ; also to Wakefield, Leeds, York, Hull and all parts of the North of England and Scotland.

" Rd. Robinson, agent."

15. Huddersfield Canal in the Colne Valley.
From a Banner worked by Florence E. Lockwood.

In passing, it is worth noticing that their competitors, the " carriers by land," despatched waggons daily, or rather nightly, to London, Manchester, Kendal, Leeds, etc.

The other immediate effect of the canal was that it encouraged the introduction of the steam engine, not only by providing a site to which coal could be transported direct from a distance, but by affording sufficient water for raising steam. At last there was the possibility of running a mill independent of the river ; but the choice of site was restricted to the canal banks. So there began another industrial " ribbon " development alongside of the older one on the river banks. It is no wonder that the two jointly led to industrial congestion in the Colne Valley, that is repeated on the other side of the tunnel through Stanedge. The corridor also stimulated the spread of cotton spinning down the Colne Valley.

Of the mills lower down the Colne, nearer Huddersfield, Parson in 1834 (*History of Leeds*, etc.), stated that in the township of Golcar and Lockwood there were then twelve water wheels of 170 horse power in all, and three engines of 57 horse power. At Milnsbridge there were four water wheels of 45 horse power and two steam engines of 6 horse power.

(3) **EVOLUTION OF THE WAREHOUSE.**

Side by side with all this expansion in the valleys, along the river and the canal and up the smaller tributaries, there was a complementary adjustment taking place on the manufacturing side of the industry located in the older upland villages. These were full of small manufacturers who were descendants of the clothiers of former days, and though they continued to buy the wool, they readily surrendered the preparatory stages to the scribbling millers, and confined themselves to spinning, so long as the jenny survived, and to weaving on the hand loom. Then, some time about the beginning of Victoria's reign, the power mule began the transfer of the spinning to the mills in the valleys,[1] and the manufacturer limited himself to the weaving. Virtually the industry remained in its domestic stage, though there was a rapid increase of the wage-earning class in the manufacturing villages, to produce a commensurate output from hand looms. To what extent, at any time, the manufacturer put jennies and looms into his warehouse it seems impossible to say. There was, no doubt, considerable variation in this respect, but for many years the bulk of the weaving was put out to be done in the cottages, and the manufacturer's warehouse remained true to its name. It did not become a mill until after the middle of the century.

Woollen manufacturers bulk very large in the Directory of 1830 and they attended the Cloth Hall in large numbers ; but many of them must have occupied little more than domestic premises and must have woven there all the cloth that they took to market. From that they ranged up to considerable firms, who later built the upland mills and weaving sheds around or near their warehouse and domestic premises. In other words, the manufacturer's mill, when weaving came to be done by power, was built in the upland hamlets and villages where his weavers lived and where his own homestead was ; whereas the spinning mill grew out of the old fulling mill and the later scribbling mill, and was consequently down by the streams. Golcar, Marsh, Lindley and Outlane on the one side of Huddersfield, Almondbury and Newsome on the other, all furnish illustrations of large modern mills developed out of the clothier's warehouse. So also the history of upland centres like Shepley, Shelley, Skelmanthorpe, Lepton, Netherton and Holme, is almost entirely the story of an enterprising family in two or three generations expanding its modest warehouse into great mills and weaving sheds, though sometimes the

---

[1] From the summary of the evidence before the Commission of 1833, quoted by Sykes in his *Huddersfield*, it is clear that Arkwright's "throstle machines," driven by steam, were being used for worsted spinning at Bradley Mill by 1823. The same lad three years later " went to the steam looms," a statement that gives quite an early date for the use of the power loom in the worsted manufacture.

16. WILBERLEE, SLAITHWAITE—An Upland Weaving Hamlet.

story is complicated by the change to cotton. A small pamphlet, *John Oldfield's Recollections of Netherton* (1910), gives a description of weaving in Netherton about fifty years earlier.

"All the folks in the district were hand-loom weavers, and Tom Dyson, father of George Dyson, manufactured cloth. He had the yarn spun at Marsden, and they used to come once a week into the Square ; skeps of yarn came on carts drawn by mules. All the weavers in the Square worked for Dyson. He compelled every family to take care of their urine to scour pieces and there used to be a large tub at the top of the stairs in every chamber. . . . Old Ali fetched the urine in a four-wheeled barrel. The handloom weavers earned twenty or thirty shillings a week."

In some cases the manufacturer gathered a few hand looms into his warehouse and there formed a loom shop that was the embryo of the modern mill. In other cases the mill grew out of a dyehouse or a finishing shop. The dyehouse required a supply of water, but it could carry on with much less water than a scribbling mill, so that, if the water was soft, a dyehouse could be located towards the source of some small tributary stream or on a hill side when a spring of drift water from a pit supplied its needs. Some of these remote upland warehouses and dyehouses flourished for a considerable time, but eventually when railways brought about a fresh distribution of the industry they failed because of their remoteness. It is worth while looking at a few examples, to see their varied origin and development, especially as the surviving buildings represent a stage that is now usually submerged in the later expansion of more successful businesses.

In Kirkburton there were at least seven of the warehouse type of woollen mill, famed in their day for the making of woven stays. The high narrow buildings still stand forlorn in the village, while the old tentering rooms and long low dyehouses are down by the stream. Here were made stays, vestings, livery cloths and other kinds of " fancy goods," the yarns coming from Linfit Mill near at hand and the weaving being done in the cottages. Three or four of the warehouses moved with the times and introduced power looms, but none have expanded and most of them are extinct.

The Victoria Warehouse in Shepley, a mile or two to the south, is another and more successful example of the evolution of the manufacturer's mill from the clothier's warehouse. It began as a dyehouse on the stream and obtained its coal from the local hillside pits. The warehouse supplied cotton warp and worsted and silk weft to as many as two hundred out-weavers, who made up fancy vestings, etc. In time (about 1880–5), Jacquard power looms were introduced. In the same yard another mill, before it began worsted weaving by power, did the finishing for the first.

Skelmanthorpe, standing at the head of the Dearne valley, also was a village of clothier's warehouses, while the old scribbling mills (Hartcliffe & Cuttlehurst) were down on the stream in Denby Dale and Scissett. At Skelmanthorpe the Field family was already represented in 1770 by John Field, a clothier of Gill Gate. In 1800 his son Joseph built a warehouse and dyehouse at Garrett, where he lived, and with his three sons, Joseph, Thomas and Richard, carried on the fancy trade in waistcoatings. About the same date, 1800, another domestic manufacturer, William Marsden by name, also built a house and warehouse at Greenside.

In the eighteen-thirties the younger generation of Fields separated. Joseph remained at Garrett ; Thomas started for himself at Elm House, where he built a dyehouse and warehouse ; Richard married Marsden's daughter and succeeded to the business at Greenside. As fashions changed and the popularity of flowered vestings waned, Richard Field at Greenside turned to quiltings and skirtings, and built a new dyehouse ; in 1850 he put in an engine to drive the finishing machines and the piece dyeing machines, and in fact turned the premises into a mill. But there was neither spinning nor weaving on the premises, for the yarn was bought, and the weaving was all put out in the cottages. With the advent of a brilliant designer, T. G. Bottrill, Greenside turned to the making of shawls, and Bottrill was presently taken into partnership. Shawls required looms up to eighty inches in width that were too big for the weavers' cottages, so a shed was added to hold fifty-six hand looms. About 1880 the Greenside firm (Field & Bottrill Ltd.) patented a process for finishing sealskins woven from Tussore silk. They built up a trade with America sufficient to employ two hundred hand looms, until it was killed by the McKinley tariff of 1889. It also killed hand loom weaving, for next year power looms were installed to weave plush. Throughout the present century the firm has concentrated upon the manufacture of plush from silk, mohair and other fibres, buying its yarn from the spinners as of old. Sir Percy Jackson, who is the head of the firm of Field & Bottrill to-day, is a Field through his mother. She was the daughter of Richard of Greenside, so that Sir Percy is great-grandson of both Wm. Marsden of Greenside and Joseph Field of Garrett.

The buildings at Garrett have been converted into cottages, but Elm House has grown into Elm Mills, where the old dyehouse still exists. The descendants of Thomas Field continued the business there until after the War, when it was sold to Mr. C. V. Rigby, who retains the old name, Frank W. Field & Co., and continues the fancy trade, making Tussore silk suitings and fancy worsteds for the tropics.

Elm Mill has also thrown an offshoot that replaces the disused Garrett. This is Tentercroft Mill, built by Edwin Field, and his grandsons continue the business under the style of Edwin Field & Sons, and the firm now manufactures Angora and Mohair Pile hearthrugs, tablecovers and curtains.

Altogether, the history of the Field family at Skelmanthorpe is a very striking illustration of some characteristic features of the Huddersfield trade and the slow evolution of the manufacturer's warehouse on the uplands.

In the Colne valley there is a stream, Bradley brook, that comes down to Slaithwaite from Lingards Moor on the south. There were several mills on this stream that failed to hold their own after 1850. The most interesting is the highest one at Holt Head, for in the early century, when the Marsden road went by Blackmoor Foot, Holt Head was on the main route to Manchester. Here a dyehouse was built in 1799, and the Dyers' Arms, better known as the "White House," still stands as evidence of the one time prosperity of Holt Head, at the top of a steep bit of the old road that has not been modernised. The stream also supplied the power for two small scribbling mills, known as Upper and Lower Holt, that are recorded in the 1805 Survey of the Dartmouth estate. The mill at Lower Clough in Merrydale was just such another establishment in the moorland valley to the north of Slaithwaite, with its dyehouse, dressing shop and warehouse.

17. Upper Holme, Slaithwaite.

On the hills between Meltham and Holmfirth there are several hamlets, Upperthong, Netherthong, Oldfield and Wilshaw, that show far better than the big manufacturing villages nearer Huddersfield the conditions under which the industry was carried on a century ago. If a mill exists it developed from an old warehouse of a clothier and the weaving was done in the village. At Wilshaw there was a dyehouse as well, and doeskins, buckskins, deerskins and meltons were woven on hand looms, dyed with fustic, madder or logwood and gathered into the warehouse. Coal came from the Haigh pits at Honley, and then about 1850 the warehouse developed into a mill. It was a flourishing concern until the death of the owner in 1874. Only after that was an engine installed and power looms introduced, but the business declined until it was in liquidation in 1882.

As for Saddleworth, with its little hamlets in the hills looking to Lancashire, its woollen industry has decayed and vanished and given place to cotton spinning mills lower down towards Oldham and Stockport. Early in the nineteenth century there were two thousand hand looms weaving the best superfine broadcloths to be bought in Yorkshire, and now there are none. Castleshaw and Deanhead under Stanedge are derelict, the clothiers' houses tenantless and crumbling to ruins. " Deanhead," wrote Ammon Wrigley in 1912, " was about the last place in Saddleworth to nourish and keep alive the woollen cloth industry, which may be said to have died in the arms of the Rhodes family. . . . One goes through it to-day, silently, and thinks of the burial service."

His illustration, reproduced here by permission, from *Songs of a Moorland Parish*, shows the workshop in the cottage at Deanhead before it was dismantled about 1912. There is not a machine or a fitting in it that does not date back to 1800. Yet as late as 1905 Joseph Rhodes was here weaving broadcloth that was renowned throughout the valley for its enduring quality. Suits made of it lasted a life-time and were cut down to fit the children. On the fifty-jinny against the wall his wife span both warp and weft. Joseph Rhodes and his brother Robert (until his retirement) wove on the two hand looms ; the bobbin (or winding) wheel and portions of the warping walls and the creeling frame are also in the picture. So in this cottage at Deanhead the domestic woollen industry of Yorkshire expired.

The cottages of the hand loom weavers were complementary to the manufacturer's warehouse. Clustered in folds or facing the street, they still distinguish the upland weaving villages and hamlets. Their long upper windows, divided by thin mullions, tell the tale of looms set against them to catch the light. And as the output of slubbings or yarn grew apace, and the demand for weavers rose, the cottages added a storey to their height to hold more looms.

This chapter, like the last, has been concerned with mills, differing in situation, origin and purpose, but alike filled with machinery the property of the mill-owner. Not yet was it all driven by power, and even the machines that were, came far short in their mechanical motions of modern ideas. At every stage the machine had to be aided by skilled fingers, and many subsidiary processes were carried through by hand. Even the power-driven machines were primitive and clumsy in their material, design and structure, and slow in action. Not merely the frame, but many of the moving and running parts were of wood. Not until Victoria's reign did iron

18. Interior of the Workshop of the Rhodes Family at Deanhead.

begin to enter largely into the structure. John Brooke (1794–1878), looking back at the end of a long life, could write :—

> " I recollect when very little iron was used in mill work. All water wheels and shafts were of wood, and boulder stones were used for shafts to run on ; but boulder stones were only seen in very old mills. I believe I am not wrong in saying that the mills at Armitage Bridge were about the first in the neighbourhood of Huddersfield where iron was generally used for wood." [1]

There is abundant evidence detailed in Chapter XII. of the transformation wrought by him and his brother in this respect between 1825 and 1850. But only exhibits of old machines themselves, as in the Tolson Memorial Museum, can effectively bring home the primitiveness of the equipment of the early mills. The pity of it is that so few of them have survived.

CHAPTER X.

THE MERCHANT-MANUFACTURER AND THE FACTORY.

As sketched in the last two chapters, the coming of machinery and power had neither convulsed nor disorganised the domestic industry. The scribbling mill had fitted itself into the existing organisation, and performed a public service that benefited the humblest clothier, and appeared to secure his position. But there were more profound consequences. For one thing the industry was in a state of flux. The success of innovations and the ever-present example of cotton mills stimulated experiment and personal adventure in new directions. For another it was brought home to the master manufacturer that workpeople could with advantage be brought together to operate hand machines under one roof on a larger scale than hitherto. Further, as scribbling mills multiplied, the manufacturer was able to employ more spinners and weavers and his increased output brought him more capital, provided that his market was also expanding. From Aikin's report on the Huddersfield trade in 1794 it is clear that this condition was satisfied, and the American market continued to be a good one for the next fifteen years. Aikin also shows that the manufacturer was alive to improving the quality of his cloth by using Spanish wool, and to increasing the variety of his products by making " fancy " cloths, which either used the new mill-spun cotton warp, or reflected in other ways the stimulus of the varied cotton fabrics coming on the market.

All this ferment of new methods and new ideas was certain to react upon the whole structure of the industry and to lead to its reorganisation upon fresh lines. For the moment there were three units in the industry—the fulling and scribbling miller, the clothier or manufacturer, and the merchant, and of these the clothiers were by far the most numerous. All of them continued to function

[1] Obituary reprint in the Huddersfield Public Library.

separately for many years, but there were exceptions from the start. From the sixteenth century the prosperous clothier, such as John Armytage of Farnley Tyas, had aimed at owning or leasing a fulling mill, and in due course this became a scribbling mill. The clothier-owner was at once in the position to reap the benefit of the use of power-driven machinery and put out more wool to be spun and woven to his order. He might even put a few jennies and hand looms into premises adjacent to his scribbling mill if he saw any reason for exercising closer supervision. Other clothiers followed his example and sought a stream site where they could erect a small mill mainly, though not exclusively, for the treatment of their own wool. It was a very natural development and it appears to be the explanation of the fact that in this district a number of firms of long standing as manufacturers, like the Wrigleys of Cocking Steps, the Nortons of Scissett and the Woods of Denby Dale, appear first as the owners or occupiers of a scribbling mill. Shortly, they all came of clothier stock, and they continued to scribble their own wool, but with the aid of power on a new site, whilst the weaving was continued on the old lines.

Neither was the demarcation between clothier and merchant as rigid as is sometimes thought. With a host of small clothiers, who sold their cloth in the balk or unfinished state, the merchant was a necessary unit in the industry. But it is not difficult at any period from Elizabethan times, to find such finishing tools as walker shears and the press in the inventories of clothiers, side by side with looms. A few of the more substantial clothiers did, in fact, dress their pieces, and probably those of their neighbours, and were merchants in all but name. This they began to adopt before the end of the eighteenth century, and so they attained a status more in keeping with the magnitude of their business and income. The name served to distinguish then from the clothiers, who were also spoken of as manufacturers, but it is now somewhat misleading, and they are better described as " merchant-manufacturers."

The scribbling mill was bound to be the pivot of any fresh orientation of the industry, for it alone contained power-driven machinery. But it was mainly the merchant-manufacturer, evolved from the clothier, who amalgamated the three branches of the industry into one organisation. When he gathered round the scribbling mill the warehouse and dyehouse of the clothier and the dressing shops of the croppers, with perhaps a few jennies and hand looms, he created a new unit that soon became known as a factory. The rise of the factory aroused considerable hostility from two quarters. The small domestic clothiers regarded it as a menace to their trade, but the greater antagonism came from the croppers, as soon as the factory owners attempted to use power for the dressing processes. This antagonism reached its climax in the Luddite Riots of 1812, when the loss of the American market had caused a slump in trade which filled the merchants' warehouses with bales of unsaleable pieces, and threw large numbers of croppers out of work. Six years earlier the opposition to factories had been sufficiently pronounced to cause the government to set up a committee of enquiry, and its *Report on the State of the Woollen Manufacture of England* throws considerable light upon the conditions at that time in the Huddersfield area.

Though croppers and clothiers made common cause against the factory owners, and had petitioned Parliament to revive certain obsolete statutes by which they hoped to check their activities, they had only one point in common—the maintenance of a seven-years' apprenticeship. Croppers or cloth-finishers had been agitating against the use of power, either in the form of gig-mills or shearing-frames, for a number of years, and had built up a strong union known as the Institution, which in Leeds had effectually prevented their introduction. But in Huddersfield the Institution had been less successful, and the local witnesses examined by the Committee were nearly all of them croppers who had worked these machines, or fine-drawers who had mended gig-dressed cloth, and one and all were hostile to their use.

Comparatively, the factory in itself aroused little opposition in Huddersfield. The Committee found that " several factories had long been established near Halifax and Huddersfield, but the principal progress of the factory system and that which chiefly created the alarm " had been in Leeds, where some very large factories had been set up since 1792. The clothiers here confined their opposition to the presentation of reports of two meetings, the one at Dobcross of the " Merchants and Master Clothiers of Saddleworth," and the other at Honley of those of the parishes of Almondbury and Kirkburton. The absence of opposition from Huddersfield is significant, and is due to the fact that the factories were largely making fancy goods and superfines, so that their competition was not being felt in Huddersfield itself or the Colne valley. The resolutions adopted at each meeting were identical, and set out (1) that the Domestic System was the one best adapted to the district and that the number of looms ought to be limited and not exceed five ; (2) the number of jennies belonging to any one person or company in his or their own buildings ought to be limited, and the number of spindles not to exceed 160 ; (3) a seven years' servitude was absolutely necessary in order to furnish good and skilful workmen.

Probably the third resolution was included merely in sympathy with the croppers, for apprenticeship amongst the clothiers was no longer obligatory, nor did the privately-owned Cloth Hall require it as a condition of membership. The two others reveal the ideal clothier, with not more than four or five jennies and looms in his warehouse or shop, enough to employ his family and one or two journeymen and apprentices ; if his business outgrew these bounds the work should be put out in the village.

The clothiers took no further steps and their forbearance suggests that no factory in the district had set up loom shops on any great scale. The croppers pushed the attack much more vigorously, from their point of view, and the brunt of it was borne by the firm of Joseph, Thomas and Law Atkinson of Bradley Mill, where most of the witnesses had worked. A few other firms are named, but only one, Messrs. John Brooke & Sons of Honley (disguised as " Mr. Brooke of Olney "), were clearly factory owners. These two were the protagonists of the contest—the merchant-manufacturers who had in some way fused the various branches of the industry into one organisation—a factory. It is desirable to see, if possible, how this had come about and what they were doing.

The history of Bradley Mill appears to begin in 1679 when William Bradley, a salter of Huddersfield, bought a house and some land in Dalton, on the river Colne, and presumably built a fulling mill there. About the middle of the next century a Joseph Atkinson (1702–72) came from Park Head in Cumberland to follow the trade of a corn and fulling miller. He leased or rented the King's Mill and Shore Foot Mill for the one and bought Bradley Mill for the other ; and close to the latter he erected a house which he named " Cumberland House," and in it set a date stone—

A
I   E
Parkhead
Cumberland
1754

The younger sons succeeded to the corn milling, and the two older ones, Joseph (1731–1807) and Thomas (1734–1813) to the fulling mill at Bradley. Perhaps Thomas soon dropped out, but in the second Joseph's time the mill would naturally develop into a scribbling mill, and in due course it passed to his sons, Law, Joseph and Thomas, who constituted the firm in 1806. Thomas was also associated with a cotton mill started at Colne Bridge (still memorable for a fatal fire in 1818), and he took an active part against the Luddites. Law Atkinson was the only Huddersfield " merchant " called as a witness before the Committee of 1806, and his evidence supplies some important facts and shows that all stages of the manufacture were carried through within the " factory," though not exclusively so.

There was first the scribbling mill handling primarily the firm's own wool, but with power enough and to spare to " work for hire for domestic clothiers." As regards weaving there were seventeen hand looms in buildings erected for the purpose and the rest was done by outweavers. There is no reference to spinning, but it is evident that there would be a similar number of jennies within the factory. The object of bringing looms within it was, he stated, " principally to prevent embezzlement, as we use Spanish wool. If we meet with men we can depend upon we prefer having them (the pieces) wove at their own houses." As merchants the Atkinsons, who were engaged in foreign trade chiefly with America and Ireland, were buying cloth from the domestic clothiers both at the Leeds Hall and in Huddersfield ; but the greater part they gave orders for—a significant fact, for it marks the beginning of the end of the Cloth Hall system.

All this cloth would be dressed at Bradley Mill, and though Law Atkinson gave little or no evidence relative to his cropping shops, the subject was fully discussed by men who had worked in them and had very reluctantly used both gig-mills and shearing-frames there. The gig-mill must have been introduced before 1784, for one witness (Richard Cockell) found it there when he went, spent twelve years raising coatings and pressed cloth with it, and had left in 1796. Shearing-frames were a more recent introduction. The first at Bradley Mill were tried in 1800, " but they did not answer their purpose and the stood till 1803," when their re-introduction caused trouble. This witness, John North,[1] stated that Atkinsons had in 1806 " twelve or fifteen boards " on which cloth was cropped by frames, and that generally they were " increasing very fast," though there were only two pairs in the district seven years earlier. " Mr. Brooks of Honley has some and Mr. Harrop of Dobcross has some."

Master and men, between them, tell the whole tale ; but its full implication is only to be seen by a comparison with the position at Leeds. There the factory of Benjamin Gott, built at Bean Ing in 1792, provided for everything to be done within its gates. The great weaving shop, four hundred feet long, filled one side of the mill yard and there was a smaller one on the other, and in 1813, with only a small addition, these contained 144 hand looms, with forty-eight jennies in the spinning room. Yet even then the finishing was all done by hand, for Gott had completely failed to introduce the gig-mill or shearing-frame. Leeds merchants were, in fact, sending cloth to be gig-dressed in Halifax and Huddersfield.

Of the factory of John Brooke & Sons at Honley at this time it is not possible to say much. The firm possesses a considerably store of old books and papers which Mr. Thomas Brooke has freely placed at our service, but very few relate to the period. Resuming their history from page 47, the second William Brooke (1704–70) migrated before 1738 from Greenhill Bank, above New Mill, to Honley, where he rented Neiley's or Crosley Mill from the Earl of Dartmouth. He even pulled down the old family home and out of the material built a house at Honley that he called " Exchange." Like his forbears he was both clothier and fulling miller. Two of his pocket books survive. The first—" Bought in Wakefield ye 13th day of January 1728 "— was used down to the year of his death and begins with the old address, " Greenhill-bank in Houlmfirth Liberty." It contains some trade entries but mainly other memoranda, such as a list of his books : Bunyan's *Grace Abounding*, Baxter's *Holy Call*, etc. The second opens with " William Brooke, Honley in the Parish of Almondbury

---

[1] He was then working at Fisher & Mallinson's and earning five shillings a day, or " some months £6 or a little better."

and County of York, Clothier. Jenu. 7th, 1738." It records continuously his purchases of wool and sales of cloth, thus :—

			£	s	d
(Dr.)	24th Jeny 1738/9 Accounted with Mrs. Stead and I owe her to be pd in Cloth	...	£4	17	5
	24th Jeny. recd one pk. of wooll att	...	6	10	0
	1st March 1738 recd. one pk. & 8 stones att		4	15	10
	24th April Recd. one pk of wooll ...	...	6	12	6
	2nd May Recd. one pk of woðll ...	...	5	12	6
	10th July Recd. 13 Stone of Noyls and a half after . . . pr pk att		5	9	8

The Contra account on the other page :

			£	s	d
20th March 1738 Sould then to Mrs. Stead one Sad[1] Do plain att	...		2	16	8
3rd Aprill Sould one Sad Do plain att	...		2	16	8
17th April ,, two Sad Dǫ plains att	...		4	0	0

William Brooke remained a clothier, though on the tombstone of his daughter (d. 1795) he was called merchant. His son John (1734-98) succeeded to the business, doubtless expanded the fulling mill into a scribbling mill, and when his sons grew up founded the firm of John Brooke & Sons about 1785–1790, and at his death he was described as a merchant.

These sons were William of Northgate House (1763–1846) and John of Honley. John retired first and William remains the greater figure and one typical of the time—a blend of squire and merchant, active in good works. He built Northgate House for himself in 1812–13, and Northgate Mount on his retirement in 1825.[2] These residences, set in their parks on the valley side away from Honley, mark the rise of the successful manufacturer of the new era. About 1815 the brothers determined to build their own factory and found a suitable site at Armitage Bridge, where there was more water power and a good supply of soft water for the scouring and dyeing. So in 1819 John Brooke & Sons entered upon a new lease of life at Armitage Bridge.

The Report of 1806 throws no light whatever on the manufacturing side of the business at Honley. The tradition is that the whole of the spinning and weaving was put out all over the country side ; nor is there any reason to think that the firm set up any looms within the factory there. But besides the scribbling mills and warehouses, the firm had its dyehouse and finishing shops and into these they had introduced gig-mills and shearing-frames. James Fletcher, a fine-drawer (who had worked for Atkinsons, Brookes, and Horsfalls of Well), stated that the frame was in use at Honley in 1803 for cutting superfine goods. Certainly Brookes had a high reputation for the quality and finish of their superfines. William Cookson, a Leeds merchant, spoke of a buyer there who "had frequently challenged any merchant or cloth dresser (in Leeds) to

---

[1] A cloth described by its colour.
[2] He also built Armitage Bridge House for his son John in 1828.

produce a piece of cloth equally well dressed with those of Mr. Brooke."

There is a contemporary sales-book (1804–5) apparently the only relic of the period, which throws some light on the merchanting side of the business. It contains the accounts of customers all over the country, and in their sequence it reflects the journey of a traveller securing orders, *e.g.*, in East Anglia. The cloths named include cassimeres, coatings, corbeaus, kerseys, moleskins, superfines, and swandowns, all characteristic of the period.

The Committee of 1806 decided against all the demands of clothier and cloth-dresser alike, and recommended the repeal of the old statutes which they had sought to make effective barriers against machinery, factory and capitalist.

Perhaps the Committee was optimistic and weighed lightly the risk of unemployment and distress arising from the spread of machinery. But at least it was guided by what had happened before, and inferred that the opposition and the injury would alike die away. " Hitherto these alarms have after a time subsided, and the use of machines has been gradually established without, as it appears, impairing the comforts or lessening the numbers of workmen." Nor could it foresee all the consequences, and indeed believed " that the apprehensions of the Domestic System being rooted out by the Factory System are at present at least wholly without foundation." But even fifty years later Edward Baines said the same.

So the Committee hoped for the best, but the Fates falsified the hope. The old Acts were repealed in 1809 whilst the country was still fighting with France and was soon to be embroiled with America. The blockade cut off food supplies and destroyed the merchants' trade with New England. Food prices rose, wages fell, unemployment grew. The clothworkers, caught hopelessly in the mesh of circumstances, struck blindly at the seeming cause of their misery— the new machines—the shearing frames, and in 1812 the district was involved in the welter of the Luddite riots with all their hideous consequences.

The circumstances of the Luddite riots have often been described,[1] whilst *Shirley* has conferred undying fame upon some of the protagonists and some of the incidents in the drama. But there is still need for a description of the " hellish machinery," the " detestable shearing frames," which provoked the struggle. The gig-mill is used in a more elaborate form to-day, but the shearing frame was employed in so small an area and for so short time that not one appears to have survived, and its structure and action are now quite forgotten. There is no example of it to be seen in any local Museum, or even in the collection of historical textile machines at the National Science Museum. To understand the shearing frame it is first necessary to know how the cropper operated his shears by hand, for the machine merely reproduced his action, using his hand shears mounted in a frame or carriage. And this mode of operation

[1] As by F. Peel in *The Risings of the Luddites, Chartists and Plugdrawers*, 1880.

is almost as completely forgotten as the mechanism of the frame, for the cropper's craft is extinct. The Tolson Memorial Museum is the only one where the cropper's shears are shown with a cropping board and the fittings used to operate the shears.

Fortunately there is an excellent lithographic illustration of the interior of the cropping shop occupied by John Wood, on the river bank close to Longroyd Bridge, Huddersfield (Fig. 19). This was the hot-bed of the Luddite riots, for George Mellor, Wood's stepson, worked in it and Booth was in Fisher's shop across the way. Evidently the artist aimed at an exact reproduction of this historic storm centre and even copied the memoranda written on the beam, viz., " Hood 1799 " and " Johney Green's web June 2d. 1810."

Beyond the window on the left are packs of teasels and close by, on the table, some " handles," the small frames to contain about a score teasels above the cross-bar of each. But there is no raising or dubbing board visible unless the apprentice in the room on the right is raising the piece in front of him on one. The stock of handles appears to be stored in the rack above the long window. Midway against the wall stands a frame, " the Nelly," on which a piece could be wound from one roller to another. It was an improvement of the ancient perch (" peark ") which remained in use in Leeds, though North told the Committee that Huddersfield dressers had used the nelly for forty years. The man at it is raising a piece, not with teasels in a handle, but with a pair of wire cards not unlike the cards used for carding wool, one in each hand. More exactly he is " rowing " it with cards, and the process was either additional to teazling in the case of superfines, or in place of it with cheaper cloths. As the wires had no hooks they did not bring up the nap as much as teasels did. Rowing with cards must have been an old practice, as it was prohibited by the Act 3 Henry VIII., c. 6. There is a nelly with a pair of cards in the Museum, and Messrs. John Brooke & Sons possess another, as well as a pair of shears complete with its fittings and board.

The four cropping boards rest on stools or trestles and they are curved to the shape of the blades of the shears. The cloth was fixed in place by hooks, which are shown on the nearer boards, and it was moved after each cut or " board," falling in " cuttle " on the floor. Only the lower blade of the shears lies on the cloth, and the conspicuous heart-shaped things upon it at two of the boards are leaden weights to increase its pressure on the nap. More of them are at hand in the rack in the foreground. The upper blade was set at an angle of about 70 degrees to the other and had a wooden lever or " nog," shaped to the top edge of the blade at its junction with the bow handle. The one cropper at the shears has his left hand on this nog. A soft leather band or loop joined the nog to a hook on a block of wood that was clamped by a thumb screw to the lower blade. This furnished a fixed fulcrum so that when the cropper pushed the nog down, the upper blade was forced towards him and closed over the edge of the lower blade. The third fitting was a shaped block of

19.   Interior of John Wood's Cropping Shop at Longroyd Bridge.

wood fitting the bow and lower blade and serving as a handle to move the shears over the face of the cloth as the nap was cut. This he holds with his right hand. The action resolves itself into a depression of the nog to close the blades, which are opened again by the spring of the bow, and so a rapid alternation of the two movements was obtained with ease.

The raising and cropping were alternated and repeated as often as necessary to obtain the desired finish, and often the cloth was worked over in the wet state at some stage. This explains the action of the man with a watering can who is, as he would say, " lecking " a piece.

Turning now to the use of power, the gig-mill was a simple piece of mechanism, little more than a revolving drum, with the teasels set in a dozen parallel holders fixed lengthways along its surface. To pass over the drum the cloth was wound on a roller and transferred to another, much as in the nelly. At first only the empty roller was driven by power and when full the two had to be exchanged ; later each roller could be engaged in turn and the cloth went backwards and forwards like a typewriter ribbon ; but before 1820 Yorkshire millwrights had made the travel continuous, with the ends of the piece sewn together to form a band.

The structure and mechanism of the shearing frame may be gathered from three sources :—(1) The evidence of a Huddersfield cropper, John North, at the Enquiry of 1806 ; a description in Rees' *Cyclopædia*, 1819 ; and the specifications and drawings of John Harmar's patents, mentioned by Rees. All three prove that the frame was only a carriage to hold and actuate the existing shears. Rees' description by itself is quite clear, but he only illustrates the " perpetual " frame of the West of England. It is as follows :

"Shearing-Frame.—The most common machine used in Yorkshire is only applied to give motion to the same kind of shears as are used for cropping by hand, and is usually called the shearing-frame. At the side of the table or cushion on which the cloth is spread (*i.e.*, the cropping board), a long stool is placed, having grooves at the edges to guide the wheels of a carriage, to which the shears are affixed by their bows. There is a carriage for each pair of shears, and they are slowly and gradually moved along the stool by a cord which winds upon a roller turned by wheel-work ; and at the same time the handles of the shears are continually pulled by a cord connected with a small crank which turns round very rapidly. The direction of the cut is the lengthways of the piece of cloth, and the two pair of shears advance across the breadth of the piece until a whole breadth is cut ; the machine is then stopped, the shears removed, and the piece of cloth shifted upon the table. . . ."

"The machine invented by Mr. Harmar of Sheffield was of this description ; his first patent was in 1787, and another in 1794. At one period his machines were in general use, but the present shearing-frames although of the same kind, are very much simplified, and work equally well."

20. OTTIWELLS MILL, MARSDEN, AS IN 1812 (now demolished).

"It should be explained that what Rees calls "the handles of the shears" (and Harmar "bobs") were the little wooden nogs. The crank was on a horizontal shaft near the floor, and as it went down to the lowest point in its revolution, the cord pulled the handle or nog down, and as it came up the nog went back and the shears opened. There seems to have been no provision for keeping the cranks vertically under their respective nogs as the shears moved across the cloth. Probably this was the reason for using two pairs so that each only travelled a short distance, though it only continued the established practice. North's description of the frames in use at Bradley Mill only differs in one detail ; according to him each frame carried "two pairs of shears.""

Apparently it was only after the expiration of Harmar's first patent that local millwrights began to utilise its two practicable ideas. Possibly at first Low Moor and Bowling ironworks displayed a willingness to make castings of frames and wheels. But certainly the frames that were smashed in the Luddite riots were made locally. There was a frame maker, John Stead, at Gomersal Hill Top, who supplied the factories in the Spen valley, or some of them, and those around Huddersfield were largely made by Enoch and James Taylor of Marsden, who soon turned their smithy into foundry and millwright's shop. That the frames were largely built of cast iron is evident, because the rioters carried a sledge hammer, which they named Enoch, crying : " Enoch hath made them and Enoch shall break them." One of these hammers from the Taylor's foundry, presented by a descendant, is exhibited at the Tolson Memorial Museum.

So the storm gathered in the cropping shops around Longroyd Bridge and broke over the district. It culminated in the night attack on Rawfolds, described in *Shirley*, and a fortnight later in the shooting of William Horsfall of Ottiwells Mill, Marsden, as he rode home from Huddersfield.

The mill in which William Horsfall had installed frames was guarded by soldiers and had been put in a state of defence by placing cannon behind a stout wall to command the approaches. The illustration (Fig. 20) shows this wall on the left with the loopholes in it, three feet by ten inches. Ottiwells Mill is now only a name and there is nothing to be gained by repeating an oft-told story, for the whole drama lives again in the opening chapters of *Inheritance*.

CHAPTER XI.

THE CLOTH HALL AND THE HUDDERSFIELD MARKET.

Until it was destroyed in 1930 the Cloth Hall stood as the emblem and memorial of the departed domestic woollen industry. For many years it had outlived its purpose, but its removal adds to the difficulty of realising what the Cloth Hall meant in the life of Huddersfield for over a century, within which the town sprang from obscurity into a municipal and parliamentary borough and the seat

21. The Cloth Hall, the White Hart Inn and Market Street, *c.* 1800.

of a great textile industry. The first step was taken when the lord of the manor, Sir John Ramsden, received from Charles II. in 1671 a charter for a market. After that Huddersfield definitely displaced Almondbury, and an open-air market in cloth grew up around its churchyard. Perhaps it was the example of Leeds, where the second White Cloth Hall arose in 1755, that moved his grandson to provide better accommodation for the Huddersfield clothiers. At least it was an opportune moment when Sir John Ramsden, the third baronet, in 1766 erected for the purpose the large brick circular arcade that has been for generations both a familiar and a distinctive feature of Huddersfield. But if the Cloth Hall was remarkable in itself there is a greater fascination in recalling the weekly ebb and flow of trade within its secret walls, and in watching the throng of people drawn into the town each Tuesday so long as it remained the hub of the industry. Rather was it the heart of the old domestic system, for each week it sent the blood of trade pulsating through the arteries to the furthest boundaries of the wide district.

Yet, though the Cloth Hall was enlarged more than once and flourished for a full century, the seeds of its decay were sown almost at its birth. The changes in method and in organisation were not all of them, nor at first any of them, inimical to the custom of buying and selling at a Hall. Indeed the scribbling mill by its increase of output stimulated a rapid expansion of the industry, and the balance could only be redressed by a multiplication of clothiers and weavers to cope with the product of machines. So domestic clothiers were never as numerous as in the next half-century, nor could they live without the Hall. But the merchant, and particularly the merchant-manufacturer, began to find it less indispensable. He preferred to give orders for what he wanted instead of buying what he saw ; or he found it an advantage to show his cloth to his customers in a private warehouse.

This was especially true in the fancy trade where novelty and design counted for much and privacy was essential. So from the beginning of the nineteenth century there was a growing class of traders who either ceased to frequent the Cloth Hall, or only used it partially. The competition of the warehouse was not seriously felt for a time because the numbers of the domestic clothiers making plain cloths remained undiminished. So the Hall held its ground until the hand-loom weaver and the putting-out system were displaced by the power loom and the woollen mill, when it ceased to be anything more than a name.

Huddersfield in 1766 was only a small town straggling up from the bridges at Aspley to the Church and Market Cross, and along Kirkgate and Westgate towards Green Head. The Cloth Hall was built near the top of the town, behind Westgate and close to the old road leading to Longroyd Bridge and Manchester. Brick was just coming into fashion, and so it came about that the most notable Georgian building in a town of ashlar stone was of brick. Halifax can still show some examples, but they all seem incongruous, for the

103

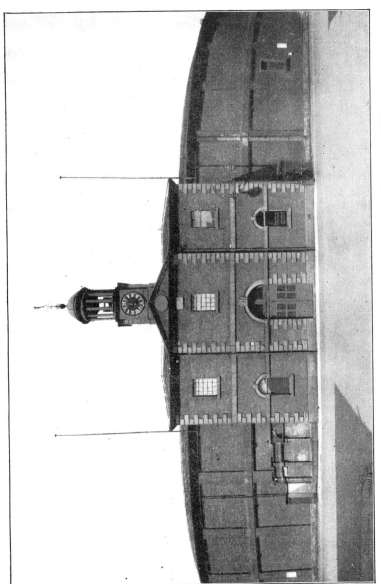

22. The Cloth Hall—Entrance from Cloth Hall Street in 1930.

Yorkshire textile towns and mills are mainly built of local stone. The Hall was also remarkable as it formed a ring or circular building round a court. In plan (Fig. 20) it was more exactly an oval or ellipse, having the longer axis of 240 ft. from north to south and the shorter, east to west, 208 ft. Along this axis was placed the important main hall, with an entrance at the eastern end. Breaking and and projecting beyond the blank outer wall of the circle this entrance block, as seen up Cloth Hall Street, was the most familiar view of the building, the cupola or open belfry and clock tower rising above the central pediment of the entrance (Fig. 19). Within this pediment was a tablet with the inscription :

ERECTED

BY SIR JOHN RAMSDEN BART.

1766

ENLARGED BY HIS SON

SIR JOHN RAMSDEN BART.

1780

A description of the building and its use, written before there were any further changes, is to be found in Edward Baines' *Directory of the County of York* for 1822, and is as follows :—

" This building, which is two stories high, forms a large circle, with a diametrical range one story high, which divides the interior parts into two semi-circles. The light is wholly admitted from within, there being no windows on the outside, by which construction security is afforded against fire and depredation. The hall is subdivided into streets, and the benches or stalls are generally filled with cloths, lying close together upon edge, with the bosom up for inspection. Here in brisk times, an immense quantity of business is done in a few hours. The doors are opened early in the morning of the market day, which is Tuesday, and closed at half-past 12 o'clock at noon ; they are again opened at 3 in the afternoon for the removal of cloth, etc. Above the door is a handsome cupola, in which a clock and bell [1] are placed for the purpose of regulating the time of commencing and terminating the business of the day."

From the date of this description it follows that the enlargement of 1780 consisted of the addition of the second storey to the circular part, as originally the whole was only one storey in height. The fabric was hardly strong enough to carry it, and the thrust caused the walls to bulge outwards to some extent. So in 1848 buttresses were built round a part of the building to strengthen it. A second tablet was inserted above the entrance to record that the Hall was

RESTORED AND ENLARGED

BY HIS GRANDSON

SIR JOHN WILLIAM

RAMSDEN BART.

1848

[1] The bell bears the inscription DALTON : FECIT : YORK : 1781.

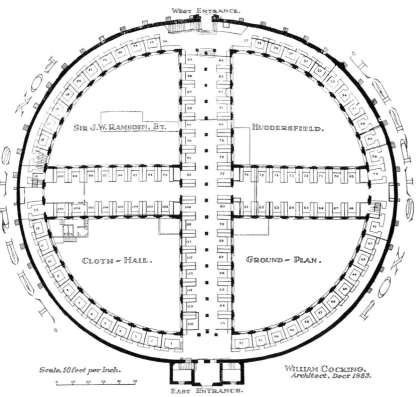

23. Plan of the Cloth Hall, as enlarged in 1864.

The enlargement can only have been a small matter, for Isaac Hordern, who entered the Ramsden Estate Office in 1846, says merely that " old Mr. Joseph Kaye was employed to build up on the south and west sides strong retaining Buttresses besides other repairs." [1]

In 1864, however, there was a real enlargement, for the so-called North and South Transepts were built along the longer axis and a handsome new entrance made at the top or western end of the main hall. The estate agent was away through illness, and resigned at the end of the year, so that Hordern was in charge of the work, and the notes from his diary are the best evidence of what was done :

" 1864. Cloth Hall North and South Transepts built and the Western Entrance. These Improvements I promoted. The cost was nearly £1300. At this time I could have let more Windows for Cloth Stands.

" Engaged with Mr. Cocking as to above 15th February."

[1] See I. Hordern's " Notes relating to the Ramsden Estate and Huddersfield." MS. (c. 1907) in the Library of the Yorks. Arch. Soc., Leeds.

The plan (Fig. 23) is the one prepared at this time by Mr. Cocking, and it shows the number of stalls renumbered and increased to 116, on the ground floor. To these should be added fifty-two or more on the upper floor of the circle.

Clearly the Hall still retained its usefulness ; so the collapse came quickly, for soon after 1870 it was nearly empty.

Internally, the circular building on both floors was divided into a large number of rooms with a window to each. They were entered from a corridor which made the complete circuit against the outer blank wall. A buyer was able to pass round rapidly and glance at the cloths exposed in each room, or at each " window," until he saw what he wanted. The main hall was different, for it was undivided except by the central row of stone pillars (Fig. 25). These with the flagged floor, the flat rush-plastered ceiling, the lofty round-headed windows on either side, gave it a dignity and a character that remained unchanged to the end. It must have presented a very animated scene when the long rows of benches, ranged in " streets," were loaded with cloth and behind them stood the manufacturers, as they called themselves, from the country : broad-spoken, rugged men from the hills such as the trade breeds no more.

So much for the Cloth Hall, within and without.[1] But to understand the part it played in the trade and in the growth of Huddersfield it is necessary to see something of the busy scenes on market day, to watch the people flocking into the town. The Cloth Hall made Huddersfield a mart where business was done not only in wool and cloth, but in all that related to them ; and it was done at inns, or up inn-yards, at street corners and in warehouses, as well as at the Cloth Hall. Nor is that all. A market town develops the mercantile side in place of the manufacturing, and it becomes a centre for allied and subsidiary trades. So banks and warehouses clustered around the Cloth Hall, though a century ago they were housed in the most modest of buildings. So also, as the merchants controlled the finishing of the cloth bought in Huddersfield, all the dressing shops and many dyehouses were congregated in the town, and it was the headquarters of the packers and the carriers, by waggon or canal, as well.

This complex organisation can be analysed by the aid of one or two contemporary directories. The most useful are Baines' (1822) already named and the *Directory of Leeds and the Clothing District* by Parson & White, 1830. They contain, to begin with, instructive lists of the country clothiers, the first one under the title of " Woollen Manufacturers from the Country who attend the Cloth Hall, with their Places of Abode, and Inns-Houses in Huddersfield." This alone tells a tale of days that are gone. In the 1830 list nearly five hundred manufacturers were named and arranged under their villages.

---

[1] The most interesting relics of the Cloth Hall are now incorporated into a shelter erected in the grounds of the Tolson Memorial Museum. The Western Entrance has also been re-erected as a gateway near the Lodge in Ravensknowle Road. (See Handbook VII.)

24. THE CLOTH HALL—THE MAIN HALL AND THE CIRCLE FROM THE COURT, 1930.

25. THE CLOTH HALL—INTERIOR OF THE MAIN HALL, 1930.

Family groups of threes and fours only occupied one stand or room in the Hall, and there only appear to have been 148 stands in all prior to the enlargement of 1864. The names are all such as are common now, and were to be found in earlier times—Sykes, Haigh, Dyson, Taylor, Broadbent, Beaumont, Brook, Ramsden, Crowther ; not a hint of immigration. Golcar sent the largest number, 101, that included eight John Taylors and seven Joseph Taylors, also a Mary Whittle. Others that ran into double figures were Meltham 62 (with more Taylors), Saddleworth 49, Holmfirth 45, Linthwaite 32, Honley 28, Slaithwaite 17, Netherthong 16 and Marsden 10. The most distant places were Skelmanthorpe 2 and Penistone 2. Each manufacturer had two numbers attached to his name ; the one of his stand at the Cloth Hall, and the other indicating his inn, where he baited his horse and dined himself.

Reference has been made in previous chapters to the rise of a new line of " fancy goods " in the Huddersfield industry, under the stimulus of the Lancashire cotton industry. The directories carry the story much further. In 1822 there was a list of 102 names of " Manufacturers of Fancy Goods who attend Huddersfield Market, with their places of abode and Inns or Warehouses in Huddersfield." Their warehouses were small rooms in yards near the Cloth Hall ; chiefly Lumb's warehouse or yard and Kilner's and Tinner's yards, in Cloth Hall Street, and Robert's court in Market Street. None of them was using the Cloth Hall ; the fancy trade was breaking with the old traditions in this as in other respects. It also occupied a definite geographical area to the east and south-east of Huddersfield. Its strength lay around Kirkheaton (twelve manufacturers), Dalton 5, Almondbury 24, Lepton 19, and Honley 8, but it continued southwards to Shepley 5, Cumberworth 5, Skelmanthorpe and Denby Dale.

By 1830 the vogue of the warehouse had increased considerably and had spread to the woollen manufacturers, who numbered half of the whole list of 255 names. Some of them came from outlying Halifax townships, as Elland, Greetland and Stainland (including John Shaw & Sons), that had now been attracted to the Huddersfield market and had their rooms in the White Hart yard off Market Street. But as many as thirty-six woollen manufacturers from Golcar were using rooms, though a few of them (as Hannah Hall & Son) were also on the list for the Cloth Hall. There were others from the Colne valley who used warehouses in Brook's yard between Westgate and Market Street, whilst Saddleworth manufacturers (19) favoured the George Inn yard.

The fancy goods area remained much as in 1822, though the trade had grown stronger in the south around Skelmanthorpe, and Honley with twenty-four fancy against twenty-eight woollen manufacturers had gone decidedly over to the newer lines. Huddersfield also was now divided.

But there was also by 1830 another clearly defined area to the north of Huddersfield engaged in a different branch of the fancy

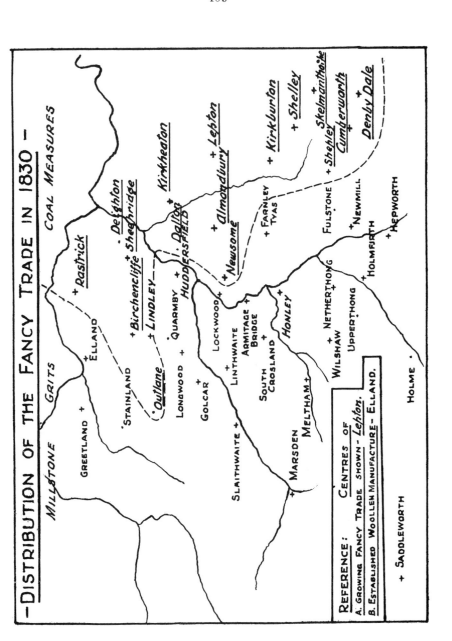

DISTRIBUTION OF THE FANCY TRADE IN 1830

COAL MEASURES

MILLSTONE GRITS

+ Rastrick

. Deighton

+ Birchencliffe + Sheepridge

+ LINDLEY

Kirkheaton

. Dalton
+ HUDDERSFIELD
+ Quarmby

+ Lepton

+ Almondbury

+ Newsome

+ Kirkburton

+ Shelley

+ Shepley
Cumberworth

Skelmanthorpe

Denby Dale

+ FARNLEY TYAS

+ FULSTONE

+ NEWMILL

+ HEPWORTH

+ HOLMFIRTH

+ NETHERTHONG

+ WILSHAW   + UPPERTHONG

HOLME .

· Outlane

LONGWOOD +

GOLCAR +

ELLAND +

· STAINLAND

GREETLAND +

+ LOCKWOOD

LINTHWAITE +

ARMITAGE
BRIDGE +

SOUTH
CROSLAND +

HONLEY +

MELTHAM +

SLAITHWAITE +

MARSDEN +

REFERENCE :   CENTRES OF

A. GROWING FANCY TRADE SHOWN - Lepton.

B. ESTABLISHED WOOLLEN MANUFACTURE - Elland.

+ SADDLEWORTH

trade. Deighton and Sheepridge appear to have taken to woollen cords and velveteens even in 1822, and by 1830 this class of goods was being made at Lindley, Birchencliffe and Outlane as well. Huddersfield was participating in it, so that the fancy trade had grown to occupy an outer ring on the north and east that just touched Huddersfield and Honley (see Fig. 26). It is remarkable that this fancy trade area is coincident with the Lower Coal Measures, whilst the Grit country continued to make plain woollens, the underlying reason being, as shown previously, that the factories equipped with steam engines were making fancy goods.

Naturally most of the warehouses were located in the inn yards, or in premises close at hand. The many inns clustered around the Market Place, or lining Westgate and Kirkgate, with their long yards, their stabling, their ranges of out-buildings, were a necessary adjunct to the business of buying and selling cloth, and they were thronged on market day. "Accommodation for man and beast" was no meaningless formula. The merchant riding in from Leeds, the small manufacturer on his nag or afoot, the carrier's waggon, the market coach, all turned into the inn-yard. Each man coming to market was to be found at his inn ; there appointments were made and bargains struck.

Time has swept away many of these old rambling yards with their muddle of stables and stockrooms, of stairs and passages. Merchants and manufacturers of a later generation lined the streets of a newer Huddersfield with the facades of their stately warehouses. But for those who search there are still relics of the old days to be found. Fortunately, before it gave way to modern improvements, the yard belonging to the King's Head in Cloth Hall Street was sketched by H. Bishop in 1923, and his water colour is now exhibited at the Tolson Memorial Museum. The reproduction (Fig. 27) shows what these yards were like, with the manufacturers' warehouses on either side let off in single rooms approached by steps and balconies. Access into the yard was through the large doors below the King's Head in Cloth Hall Street ; and the King's Head was below the White Hart at the corner of Market Street shown in Fig. 21. More than any other, the King's Head was the resort of the fancy manufacturers, for here came many from Almondbury, Dalton, Lepton, Kirkheaton and Honley.

At this time the Leeds merchants were the chief buyers at the Huddersfield market, apart from the local merchants who were mostly of the type already described, merchant-manufacturer. Among the latter were Norris, Sykes & Fisher of The Well and of Marsden, who had succeeded to A. & J. Horsfall at Ottiwells Mill ; W. & J. Whitacre of Woodhouse ; W. W. & A. Stables of Chapel Hill ; Starkey, Buckley & Co. of Longroyd Bridge ; Joseph Armitage & Co. of Milnsbridge ; Harry Brook & Sons of Well-house ; and John Brooke & Sons of Armitage Bridge.

At the other end of the scale were the woolstaplers and foreign wool merchants who came to sell English and Spanish and German

27. THE KING'S HEAD YARD—*C. H. Bishop.*

wool to the scribbling millers and manufacturers. Though there is a list of sixty in the 1830 Directory, most of the woolstaplers were firms in Leeds, London or elsewhere, who sent representatives to market or had agents in the town. There was no trade in woollen yarn, but one or two worsted spinners of Bradford had agents here, to supply the needs of the fancy trade. Besides these account has to be taken of the drysalters, such as Jas. Roberts & Co., for the supply of oil and dyewares to the trade, and the merchants of woad and teazles. The supply of these came largely from the neighbourhood of Selby, though Somerset sent large quantities of teazles to Leeds, which was the chief market for both. Joseph Hick in Westgate was the local dealer.

As for the allied and subsidiary trades located in Huddersfield, the cropping shops were the most important. There were many of them, in the town around Longroyd Bridge, in Outcote Bank, Westgate, Northgate and Croppers Row ; or further out at Paddock and Birkby. Nearly a hundred master cloth-dressers were named in the 1820 Directory, and a dozen fine-drawers ; but by 1830 their numbers had dwindled to little more than half. The dyehouses were mostly on the river side, as were two or three mills for cutting or grinding dyewoods such as logwood.

Apart from Enoch Taylor at Marsden little is heard of machine makers, as the woollen industry, in comparison with cotton or worsted, as yet afforded little scope. Away at Dobcross in Saddleworth a mechanic's shop developed out of a smithy by Joseph and John Platt, was in 1822 the embryo of the great firm at Oldham.[1] In Huddersfield Benjamin Carter had his brass and iron foundry in Quay Street and was a machine maker and millwright, and in 1830 there were several more at Longroyd Bridge. The more ancient crafts, however, were more in evidence, and Huddersfield had it shears makers and grinders, its shuttle makers, its slay and heald makers.

The most interesting of these early subsidiary industries is card-making. Though scribbling mills displaced the ancient hand-cards, they required similar " card-clothing " to cover the revolving cylinders of the machines. The enormous increase in the demand for cards, both for wool and cotton, caused an expansion in the industry of card-making, but did not alter its method of production. For many years the wire was cut and bent and the staples fixed into the leather sheet or garter by hand. This last, called card-setting, was put out to be done by women and children at home. Easther noticed them at work at Mirfield. " In driving through that village in 1840–44, the traveller would notice numbers of women sitting on the doorsteps of the cottages with long perforated straps of leather across their knees, into which they stuck with great accuracy wires bent for the purpose." The rate of pay was a halfpenny for setting 1,450 staples, a task that took about two hours.

---

[1] In 1816, John Platt & Sons were "machine makers and joiners" : nor did castings take the place of wood in the framework of machines until about 1830.

The industry also remained extremely localised, between Halifax on the west and Cleckheaton, Liversedge and Mirfield on the east. In 1816 Kirkheaton had a cardmaker, John Armitage by name, and later Ann Armitage & Sons carried on the business. Others came to the Huddersfield market, but the most important local name is that of John Sykes of Lindley, who before 1810 had started the business that grew into Joseph Sykes Brothers of Acre Mills, Lindley, one of the firms composing the English Card Clothing Co. The family had come to Lindley from Elland, where John Sykes of Ainley Top was apprenticed to John Bray, a cardmaker of Elland, in 1761.

CHAPTER XII.

TO THE GREAT EXHIBITION OF 1851.

The Great Exhibition of 1851, the apotheosis of the Industrial Revolution, may well serve as the goal of this voyage down the centuries. It was the fitting climax of a period in which invention and applied science had with ever-increasing impetus swept the nation along, without vision of the port or guidance at the helm. It marked the triumph of machinery and power ; it was the expression of England's pride in its ability to supply the world with its manufactures in iron and cotton and wool, and of its belief in Free Trade.

But this triumph had been won at a heavy price. Growth of population and its haphazard concentration in new manufacturing towns, without efficient government or sewerage or adequate water supply, brought overcrowding and slum conditions, with cholera and high mortality in their train. Child labour was used without restrictions ; hours of labour were long and unregulated ; factory inspection unknown, wage-earners without rights and trade unions illegal. By the time of Peterloo (1819) the manufacturing districts were hot-beds of social evils and for another decade or more these multiplied unchecked.

Behind it all lay apathy on the part of the State, ignorance and brutality in the masses, and an utter absence of ideals of public health or local administration. Then slowly from that time apathy began to give place to a consciousness of the need of reform. Constant agitation, sometimes threatening and sometimes ill-directed, compelled the State to set about the reform of Parliament and of effete Corporations. Guided and inspired by the dauntless sympathy of philanthropists and manufacturers, like Wilberforce and Shaftesbury, Richard Oastler of Fixby Hall, Michael Sadler, John Wood of Bradford and John Fielden of Todmorden, it compelled attention to social evils and created public opinion. Royal Commissions followed and laid bare the iniquities and horrible conditions of life in the industrial towns, in mines and in factories.

The first sign of the change in spirit came in 1824 when the right of combination was restored to the wage-earners ; and the next quarter-century down to the Great Exhibition becomes an epoch of achievement in the domain of social welfare. The dawn came with three great Acts affecting as many spheres of the national life. The Reform Act of 1832 at least swept away for ever the rotten boroughs and put the new industrial towns upon the political map. The Municipal Corporations Act of 1835 swept out the close corporations, laid the foundations of modern local government and gave the ratepayer a vote. The Factory Act of 1833 put the children under the protection of the State, excluded the youngest and threw the factories open to inspection. It is easy to see that none went far enough, but they opened three long vistas of reform which we now view from the other end. "At last," writes Professor Trevelyan, " the ice-age of English institutional and corporate life had come to an end, and the life of the community began to be remodelled according to the actual needs of the new economic society."

Throughout the forties legislation continued to respond slowly but surely to the demands of the towns. The Chartists alone achieved nothing directly for they were crying for the moon. The Ten Hours Day, for which Oastler, the " Factory King," had fought strenuously from 1830, was not won till 1847 ; but by an earlier Act in 1844 factory children under thirteen became half-timers and as such had to attend school the other half of the day—the first step towards universal education. In 1846 Cobden saw the triumph of his Anti-Corn Law League, when Sir Robert Peel abolished the duties on foreign corn ; and two years later the Puolic Health Act inaugurated the long-delayed work of sanitation. So by the middle of the century England had grappled with the problems born of the industrial era, and had in some degree put her house in order.

To state the social evils that the Industrial Revolution had brought in its train is not a condemnation of the mill-owners. Neither the employers of labour nor the politicians must be judged by the standards of life to-day. Child labour was no new thing, and long hours of labour were not new. Children suffered from brutality at home as they did in the mill or the pit; but there were good masters as well as bad, and the exploitation of child labour by the wholesale importation of pauper apprentices, was nearly confined to the early cotton mills and was checked in 1802. Factory control and inspection were regarded as an interference with individual rights by perhaps the majority of mill-owners. But it must be remembered that the first real Factory Bill was introduced into the House by two mill-masters, Robert Owen and the first Sir Robert Peel, in 1815 ; and that when the first effective Factory Act was passed in 1833, its provision of government inspectors had been suggested and urged by mill-owners.

There are excuses to be found even for the failure of the State to grapple with the problems. The French Revolution had put fear of Jacobinism into the hearts of the politicians and caused a harsh repression of all agitation here. The wars with Napoleon and America delayed due consideration of domestic affairs. The House of Commons was filled with scions of the aristocracy and landed gentry. What could they, conscious only of the amenities of their own estates, know of the conditions of life in the new industrial towns ? Political reform had to precede all other reforms.

The new middle classes were almost as powerless as the working classes. Who was there to build cottages for the workpeople except mill-owners with what money they could spare from their business ? Who was there to make streets and provide sewers, or to control the growth of a town, that had only a vestry and a village constable for its government ? There were not even the materials for cheap buildings and efficient sewers. Public opinion was most sluggish of all about sanitation. It was good enough to turn mill refuse and town sewers into the nearest stream. The whole science of sanitation had to be created and civil engineering brought into being and local government developed, before the problems produced by the Industrial Revolution and the increase of population could be solved. The solution was one of the glories of the Victorian Age. Now we are discovering that the problem of slums is not merely a material one, but a personal one as well.

Within this national framework come all the movements that agitated Huddersfield, and they can be best understood when regarded as part of the whole. The growing town was not yet a municipal borough, but the numerous parliamentary elections that came after 1832 were immensely educative and formative in spite of the narrowness of the franchise, because Oastler kept the cause of the factory children to the front. The town produced public-spirited men by whose efforts Huddersfield College was founded in 1838, and the Mechanics' Institute started on its educational course in 1843. George Jarmain taught Chemistry at both and did no little to arouse a sense of the value of chemical science and its applications in the dyehouse. But earlier than Jarmain was John Nowell of The Wood, Farnley Tyas, teacher of Jarmain and friend of Dalton. John Nowell (1794–1869), a manufacturer and dyer at Birks Mill, Almondbury, was the first to probe the mysteries of the dye vat and to experiment with his dyes and mordants in place of following the rule or thumb. He and Jarmain laid the foundations of Huddersfield's dyestuffs industry that was developed after the discovery of mauve in 1856 by Thos. Holliday and Dan Dawson, pioneers in the production of colours from coal-tar. Equally notable was the earlier work of the founder of the firm, Read Holliday, who in 1830 commenced the distillation of ammonia from gas liquor, and so gave the trade a new and cheap scouring agent.

The development of Huddersfield was by no means so haphazard as of other towns, for its expansion was subject to the control of Sir John Ramsden and the trustees of his grandson, that ensured a uniformity and an orderly laying out of the town that were quite exceptional. James Smith was able to tell the Royal Commission of 1844 that in Huddersfield " the late Sir John Ramsden did much for the ample width and proper arrangement of the streets, and construction of sewers ; and upon the whole the streets are well arranged, of ample width, well paved or macadamised, and the main sewerage has been much attended to and a more extended and complete system of sewerage is now going forward. . . .

" Notwithstanding . . . much remains undone ; and there are in Huddersfield, as in other towns, many unpaved streets, many without sewers, and a considerably extent of damp and filth in the streets, courts and alleys ; and in such localities fevers and a lower tone of general health prevail.

" Here, as in other towns, the private courts are considered to be beyond the jurisdiction of the authorities and the cognizance of the police ; and although in many places crowded with pigsties, filthy and extensive dung-hills and open privies, they are permitted to remain a nuisance to the neighbourhood and excessively injurious to the health and comfort of the inhabitants themselves ; and although each individual complains of the nuisance caused by his neighbour, he refuses to remove the nuisance caused by himself."

THE WOOLLEN MILL.

All this ferment, all these changes that mark this quarter-century were the reactions of the nation to the new economic and social conditions. Meanwhile, the woollen industry was reshaping itself and adjusting itself to steam and mechanism. The factory of 1825 was far from being a woollen mill in the modern sense. Spinning and weaving were still done by hand, and mainly off the premises. The out-workers were numerous and scattered, working in their own homes and with their own tools. Even slubbing, within the mill, was done on a hand machine. Nor did the interior present the appearance of a modern mill. There was neither the speed nor continuity of running, and above all else the machines themselves were still clumsy-looking structures or frames of wood, lacking all the grace of design and adaptation that came later as the machine-maker and the engineer took them in hand.

Once again, the Great Exhibition is significant, for it marks the completion of the evolution of the woollen mill. Within the quarter-century, or nearly so, every process had been brought into the mill and every operation could be performed by power. The sheets of the six-inch Ordnance maps of 1854 are dotted with " woollen-mills." It took another quarter-century for the power loom to displace the hand loom, and in the fifties it was only the most advanced firms who had accepted all that the machine maker could offer them. In the fancy woollen trade especially the hand loom remained in use to a much later date. In Professor J. H. Clapham's words, " In 1866 the hand-weavers managed about a quarter of the looms in the trade ; they still had some importance twenty years later." [1]

This evolution of the woollen-mill can be traced in detail and with accuracy in the case of one firm, and that the largest, Messrs. John Brooke & Sons, because the private accounts of the partnership have been preserved from the year 1825, and Mr. Thomas Brooke has kindly allowed one of us to examine the record.

[1] *Economic History of Modern England*, Vol. II. (1932), p. 83.

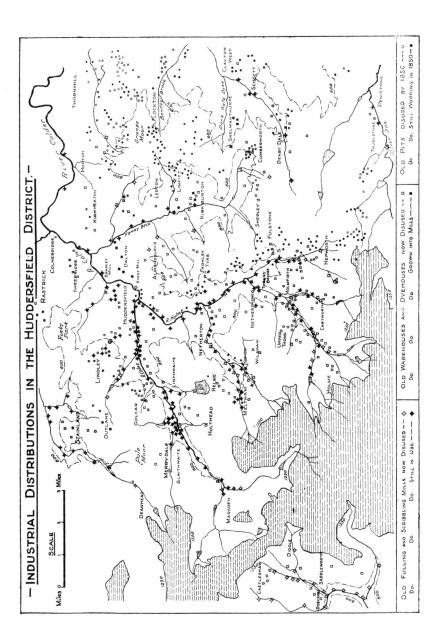

— INDUSTRIAL DISTRIBUTIONS IN THE HUDDERSFIELD DISTRICT. —

As it happens, the control of the firm passed to the third generation on the retirement of William Brooke of Honley in 1825. Two of his sons, John (1794–1878) and Thomas (1798–1859) then entered into partnership and took over all the machinery and plant of the Armitage Bridge mills, though the freehold buildings remained with their father. He also continued to provide most of the capital, and besides the fixed interest on this he drew rent for the buildings, and this was raised when further buildings were added a few years later at his expense.

So the brothers commenced what they titled the " Stock Book of John and Thomas Brooke carrying on business under the firm of John Brooke & Sons, Honley, July 1825," though Armitage Bridge is written inside the cover and the business was there and not at Honley. This Stock Book shows the annual balance sheet and what amounts to a profit and loss account, and for a long period details of expenditure upon new machinery and buildings are added. These last provide the material by which the evolution of the woollen mill may be watched.

The first year was a difficult one, for 1826 brought falling prices, bad trade and a financial crisis, but by 1828–29 the firm had added a new mill at a cost of £10,000 and filled it with machinery at a similar cost. The purchase of looms (at a cost of £750) and gear for them probably marks the introduction of weaving into the mill. The number is not stated but might be a hundred or more, as they were hand looms.[1] The " new weaving shop " is named in 1831. It is also probable that the purchase of three " power mules " (*i.e.*, self-acting) from Hewes and Wren of Manchester (£480) and more mules from Stead (£380) in 1829, mark the introduction of spinning. Three more power mules were added in 1831. Scribblers and carders might be either renewals or additional plant, but two power billies (£109) in 1829 and again in 1830 and 1831 mark an advance, for up to then the billy had been worked by hand. Power was also applied to the finishing plant all round ; to gigs, presses, brushing mills, but especially to Lewis shearing frames or cross-cutters, or variants of them. It is noteworthy that Benjamin Gott & Sons at Leeds were also introducing mules and gigs, and probably the Lewis cross-cutter this same year 1829 ; though Wm. Lupton & Co. of Leeds bought their first Lewis machines in 1823.

It is possible that the partners had started with a new equipment of some cross-cutters in 1825, but the first clear indication is the purchase of two Lewis knives (£160) in 1828, followed next year by four Marshall knives (£120) and two " Davis cutters with

[1] Definite evidence that the " principal factories " of the district at this date were weaving on the premises, is afforded by a contributor (" K ") to the *Leeds Mercury*, whose second letter on the " Woollen Manufacture " appeared 12 December, 1829. He was concerned with the unemployment caused by bad trade, and in his analysis of the position he gives the total number of looms in various factories (un-named) as 52, 67, 70, 130 and 147 respectively. In the last (where 115 were working in daylight and only 32 standing) the men had not earned more than 10/- or 11/- per week for seven months owing to short time.

additional cutters to old machines " (£250) ; with others in succeeding years. There is an old controversy underlying these entries. The position was that J. & W. Lewis, a firm of clothiers in Gloucestershire, had in 1818 obtained a patent for " Improvements in Shearing Machines," in conjunction with Wm. Davis, their engineer at Brinscomb, who assigned his interest in it to them. This, the Lewis cross-cutter, was a rotary machine, cutting the cloth from list to list. But the idea of a spiral rotary action was in the air, and it seems certain that Davis had previously seen it applied to a machine in London and passed the idea on to his employers, who had taken out their first patent in 1815. Meanwhile it had spread to America. In 1829 Lewis & Co. twice over established the validity of their patent in the courts, but Davis, who had settled in Leeds, and other Leeds firms, were making machines on the American model, and as appears from these accounts were selling them in the district.[1] Twelve more Lewis cross-cutters were purchased by Messrs. Brooke in 1830-32, and one can now be seen in the Tolson Memorial Museum. The first perpetual cutters working the length of the cloth was introduced in 1838, and the Museum also has an example of this type.

Additions and renewals continued regularly year by year. In 1832 there was need of more power, and a 40 h.p. engine and two boilers supplied by the Low Moor Company were installed in new buildings at a cost of £3,500. Then in 1836 came the first provision of power looms ; six broad looms at £22 and six narrow at £18 were set up in one room of a new building. Two years later a power loom mill was built at a cost of £3,000 and fifty looms bought from E. Leach of Rochdale (six narrow at £18, forty-three broad looms for plains at £22 and one broad loom for Kerseys [2] at £21) and four more added the next year. Other additions at this time were twelve mules of three hundred spindles each at 4/6 per spindle ; while " traversing gigs " one year were followed by " hand-raising machines " and two hand-raising shops the next, so that some kinds of cloth were still being raised by hand.

In 1842 there were thirty-eight new power looms, and two with Jacquards, which mark a further stage ; but though more looms were soon added no more Jacquards appear until 1852, when eight were installed followed by twenty more in 1854. These afford evidence that the firm was turning to some branch of the fancy trade and weaving patterned cloths. The purchase of ten " Chevalier's patent fulling stocks " at a cost of £595 in 1846 marks the introduction of the first rotary milling machine, which had been put on the market in 1843.[3] There are one or two other changes to note before the mid-century. In 1836 a warehouse was built in Huddersfield at a cost of

[1] See *Leeds Mercury*, 28 November and 12 December, 1829, 23 January, 1830.
[2] Broad Kerseys are shown in the Pattern Book of Richard Hill, 1770. See *Making Place in Soyland*, by H. P. Kendall, Hlx. Ant. Soc., 1916, p. 17.
[3] See Chevalier's advertisements in the *Leeds Mercury*, October-November, 1843.

£4,000, and 1849 affords the first evidence of purchases of wool in Australia.

The early fifties brought a number of novel machines—Oldfield's piecing machines, patent feeders, warping mills, warp-drying machines, and most notable of all the first condenser (Cotterell's) in 1853, soon followed by others. This meant that the slubbing billy was doomed. The old waggon boilers were also being pulled out and replaced by Cornish boilers.

Bald as the story is and presenting only one aspect of a progressive and successful firm for a generation, it does emphasise the point that the evolution of the mill has been continuous. Only the time-limit ends the recital, but it has gone far enough to show the complete passage from the early factory to the modern type of mill. It was the work of one generation (William Brooke had distributed his capital amongst his family in 1841 and died in 1846). The sons of Thomas Brooke began to come into the business from 1854, and after his death in 1859, and John's retirement in 1861, two of them entered into partnership and began the course of the fourth generation which carried it on into the present century.

THE FANCY TRADE.

The financial crisis of 1826 was followed by years of bad trade and low prices in the industry generally. In July 1826, according to the *Leeds Mercury*, the unemployed of Saddleworth were working on the roads two days a week and receiving twelve pounds of oatmeal for a day's work. In August 2,500 families in Huddersfield were in receipt of relief and by November, 3,500 in the township of Delph (Saddleworth) were on the list of paupers. In Almondbury four hundred "operative manufacturers," *i.e.*, weavers, were receiving support from the relief committee, for the depression had almost extinguished the fancy trade of Almondbury, Dalton, Kirkheaton and Kirkburton.

There was a temporary improvement next year, and the accounts of Messrs. J. Brooke & Sons show no further sign of the depression. But the *Leeds Mercury* throughout 1829 reflects both it and the consequent distress which came to a head in that year. It was again most acute in the districts engaged in the fancy trade, and in response to a meeting at Almondbury the masters or manufacturers undertook an investigation of the distress. The committee in its report found that in the most impoverished class where the wage-earner was not bringing home more than 2/- per week per head of his family, there were over 13,000 people out of a population of twenty-nine thousand, who had to subsist on 2½d. per day per head. Another investigation in Huddersfield found the "fancy stuffers" to be worst off and then the outdoor "woollen manufacturers" (weavers). "The people in the neighbourhood of factories were best off, as comfortable as in 1825, for the proprietors had not followed the abominable system of reducing wages ; clothiers in the neighbourhood of factories also gave adequate wages."[1]

[1] *Leeds Mercury*, 19 September and 12 December, 1829.

The *Leeds Mercury* continued to give much prominence to the conditions in Huddersfield, and on 2nd January, 1830, gave a full retrospect of the " State of the Trade in the District of Huddersfield," believing that the reports of its able correspondent justified the conclusion that trade had begun to improve. Several facts emerge from this that are of value. Thus in August, while the reports showed the fancy trade still " extremely depressed " there were better sales at the Cloth Hall week by week until on August 22nd " more woollen goods were sold in that place last Tuesday than on any one market day since the autumn of 1827. The quantity bought by the Leeds merchants alone overloaded four stage waggons and amounted in weight to at least sixteen tons." It is a graphic description that deserves to be brought to light again after a century ; and to complete the picture a later report (4 December) supplies the number of pieces. " The quantity of pieces of woollens sold in Huddersfield market to the Leeds merchants, who are the principal buyers, in September was larger than in any month in the present year and amounted to 3,970," though in succeeding months it fell away to 3,450 and 3,020.

Turning to the fancy trade once more, the report published in the issue of 3rd October, 1829, discloses a fact that in reality marks the birth of design in the Huddersfield trade, through the introduction of a loom capable of weaving patterned cloths. " One branch of the fancy trade has, however, been considerably revived by the introduction of a machine called a *Witch*, which enables the weaver to beautify the cloth with a great variety of flowers ; and this species of goods being new is in considerable demand, and employs a proportionate number of looms."

Then on 21st November, 1829, appeared the first contribution by " K," a long letter describing the " Fancy Trade near Huddersfield." In this he set out its geographical range through Huddersfield, Almondbury and the villages southwards named in the last chapter. Fifty years after its birth the trade could employ ten thousand looms, but it had been depressed since 1825. It made use of cotton, silk, wool and worsted yarns and the manufacture fell into three branches, woollen cords, cassinets and waistcoatings, the last of which was by far the most important. Cassinets had only been made during the last ten years and wages had fallen so low that the weavers could only earn from 4s. 6d. to 3s. a week. The weaving of woollen cords was the most laborious class of work, and even a " stout athletic man " had to labour twelve to fourteen hours a day to earn 7s. 6d. a week when his winder was paid. For waistcoatings wages had been declining four years and were not then more than 7s. or 8s. a week for the cheapest class, or 12s. to 14s. for the finest work.

K's comments on the Witch loom are especially valuable. The novelty of the flowered waistcoatings had created a considerable demand in the home market, but there were not more than 280 to 300 witch looms at work. The cost of them was about £7 each, and and of this £5 was paid by the manufacturer and £2 " in the time of the weaver," *i.e.*, by the weaver out of his wages. This is the clearest and perhaps the only illustration in the woollen industry of the transitional stage between the domestic industry when the worker owns his tools and works at home, and the factory system when he does not. The employer is shown here to be bearing the greater part of the cost of the witch-loom, though it was not on his premises. In other words, he bought the loom and then hired it to the weaver, at least for a period.

From this point the story may be continued by the aid of two papers in the first volume of the *Journal of the Yorkshire College Textile Society* (1889-1890). The one is an obituary notice of Professor John Beaumont, by his son and successor in the chair, Professor Robert Beaumont ; the other is an article on " The Jacquard Machine," in which, shortly before his death, the elder Beaumont described what he knew of its introduction into Huddersfield. John Beaumont was appointed to the Chair of Textile Industries in 1875, a year after the Yorkshire College (now the University of Leeds) was opened, but he had previously spent all his life in Huddersfield as a designer in the fancy trade. He was born at Lepton in 1820, his father being a small manufacturer of fancy woollens which he designed himself. Almost his earliest recollection, when he was not more than eight years old (*i.e.*, 1828-9), was seeing in motion " a loom constructed on the drum witch principle employed to some extent to lift and depress the warp yarns before the invention of the modern type of dobbie." He made his first pattern, a figured hair-line, on either a witch or a dobbie loom. But at eighteen he sought a position elsewhere, " for it was evident to him that his father would never profit by his work, because every pattern he produced was in a few days in the hands of their competitors." After varied experience in the district John Beaumont about 1849-50 joined James Tolson & Sons of Dalton as " designer of figured goods on both harness and dobbie looms," and was instrumental in the firm's success at the Great Exhibition, where they were awarded a gold medal for fancy woollens.

Clearly Professor Beaumont's experience qualified him to write with knowledge of the fancy trade from the inside. So of the Jacquard, after a reference to its introduction into the damask trade of Halifax in 1827 (this was by James Akroyd of Old-lane), he tells how a Frenchman came to Huddersfield in 1830 or 1831 and invited the manufacturers to inspect a Jacquard machine on exhibition at the George Inn. They were slow to go. John Wood of Joshua Wood & Sons, Dalton, went and was favourably impressed ; so he asked Charles Oldfield, a noted loom and witch maker, to have a look at it. But Oldfield did not like it at all.

" This supineness," writes Beaumont, " may be attributed to the fact that there were in the Huddersfield district at that time two classes of machines for producing figured vestings. One was the Drum Witch and the other the Engine (or Dobbie). The largest machine constructed on the drum principle would have a capacity of about forty (heald) shafts, but was at this time losing its hold in consequence of the clumsiness of its appearance ; while the Engine, with a weaving capacity ranging from twenty-four to 160 shafts, was fast coming into favour. The latter machine was invented by the late Joseph Senior, of the firm of George Senior & Sons, Dalton, and his foreman and designer, Thos. Brooke. These two individuals were the first, so far as we can ascertain, to make use of the wire spring for the centre of the machine, and the perforated lags into which pegs were inverted for actuating the upright wires." [1]

But Professor Beaumont proceeds to tell how a manufacturer of the name of Gill, at that time in business with Joah Sugden of Woodsome Lees, decided to use the Jacquard, and erected premises at Arkenley on the south side of Almondbury.

" Mr. Gill engaged for his foreman or manager the talented but unfortunate Wm. Norton, and no sooner had they got settled in their new buildings than they entered into the Jacquard trade in the most spirited manner possible, completely eclipsing with their large and elaborate designs those makers of fancy vestings who were limited to 160 threads of warp in the size of a figure, whilst (they) had no jacquard with a less capacity than four hundred threads. The new machine having fallen into the hands of enterprising and energetic men, who employed the best designers in the trade, soon made its influence felt, compelling such firms as Seniors, Tolsons, Sugdens, Kayes, Taylors Nortons and others to adopt it, thus obtaining a position in the district which it retains to the present day, as the best machine extant for making figured goods of almost every class in endless variety."

The Museum possesses patterns of cloth of this period, and amongst them a range of attractive fancy vestings (or waistcoatings) showing the flowers and sprigs that were first made on the drum witch, then the dobby and finally on the Jacquard, as these were. This set preserves the name of a family of designers associated with Almondbury all through the last century. The first of the name Joseph Etchells (b. 1766) of Huguenot descent, left Lichfield and settled in Almondbury in 1796. Trained in silk weaving, it is possible that he introduced the idea of combining silk with wool into the district. He established himself as a small manufacturer of silk-figured fabrics. His son, William Etchells (1814–1873), became a designer, and was with George Senior & Sons of Dalton, for whom he designed all these patterns about 1846–56. Later he was with Taylor Brothers of Common Mills, for whom he designed figured silk and

[1] The claim is doubtful, except as regards Huddersfield. James (*Worsted Manufacture*, p. 374) describes how James Akroyd at Old-lane was making the stuff called dobby, a kind of figures wildbore, before 1820, by the aid of a wood machine above the loom. The stuff clearly derived its name from the machine. The figures were at first small diamonds or lozenges, called "birds-eye," and then flowers not larger than a sixpenny piece.

woollen shawls and mantle cloths. His four sons all followed in his footsteps, and the youngest, John W. Etchells, is the donor of the patterns.

It was this generation of designers who built up the high reputation of the fancy trade of Huddersfield, which the Great Exhibition of 1851 established. More than that, they largely helped to bring about the natural transition to fancy woollens and worsteds for men's suits upon which Huddersfield largely depends to-day. Even at the Great Exhibition J. T. Clay of Rastrick, Isaac Beardsell & Co. of Thongsbridge, J. & T. C. Wrigley, J. Taylor & Sons of Newsome, and Oldfield, Allen & Co. of Lockwood Mills were all showing fancy woollen trouserings.[1] Perhaps the two designers who did most to launch the fancy worsted manufacture were Patrick Martin, founder of the firm of Messrs. Martin, Sons & Co. of Wellington Mills, Lindley, and John Beaumont, whose son states that W. Learoyd & Sons of Huddersfield entered upon it in 1870 whilst he was with them. " Up to 1870 worsted cloths had been invariably piece dyed, the attempts at using fancy yarns in worsted fabrics having been chiefly confined to figured and spotted vestings."

When Patrick Martin commenced for himself in Wellington Mills it was only a small concern, and he began by making woollen cords, which he sold in the King's Head Yard. Soon he turned to the manufacture of fancy worsteds, and the high reputation of the firm, built upon his skill as a designer, has been added to by the consistent use of the finest yarns.

John Brooke & Sons began tentatively to see what they could do with worsteds about 1875. The tale goes that when William Brooke carried the first piece into the office to show to his elder brother (Sir Thomas), the latter instead of admiring it, ripped it in two, exclaiming, " What's this rubbish ? Take it away ! " However, William was not discouraged. Before long worsted combing, spinning and weaving were all well established at Armitage Bridge, side by side with the woollen manufacture.

The drift to worsted, however, has not been a strong one in Huddersfield. The modern industry is graded rather on other lines. The Fine Cloth Manufacturers' Association, deriving in the main from the older fancy trade, includes only the firms that are making high-grade suitings, whether woollen or worsted, serges and overcoatings. Auxiliary to this group are the piece dyers and finishers ; the firms that maintain Huddersfield's high reputation in the dyeing and finishing of woollens and worsteds. The Technical College has played no small part in keeping up the succession of skilled dyers trained both in the College and in the dyehouse.

Another group, even more closely related to the old fancy trade, uses a variety of fibres, and makes cords, plushes, and mohair pile cloths for upholstery and soft furnishings. Some of the old familiar names have vanished, but the Fields of Skelmanthorpe are a notable

---

[1] *Catalogue of the Great Exhibition*, 1851, Vol. II. Details of all Huddersfield firms exhibiting, extracted from the Catalogue, are given in the Appendix.

29. THE COLNE VALLEY AT MILNSBRIDGE IN 1922.—*Florence E. Lockwood.*

example of persistence in this line. Equally so is the firm of Lockwood & Keighley Ltd. of Upperhead Mills, who are still making cords, though not for the same purposes, as they were when they were awarded a Prize Medal at the Great Exhibition.

There remains a large group of manufacturers of men's tweeds of medium grade, whose mills are now concentrated in the Colne valley, where they certainly were not when the fancy trouserings from this district impressed the jury at the Great Exhibition. Clearly it is sprung from the old fancy trade, relying still upon novelty of design and the use of medium grade wools and cotton warps. It owes a good deal of its success to the experiments of John Nowell and George Jarmain in the carbonising of wool to destroy the vegetable fibres entangled in the fleeces, for the carbonising process permits of the use of a lower grade wool.

Its concentration in the Colne valley is another matter. The chief cause in bringing this about has been the railway. Just about the middle of the century Huddersfield was linked to Leeds and Manchester by its first railway, traversing the Colne valley. The low road to Marsden had done something to open out the valley, but the effect of the railway was incomparably greater, and an immense expansion of industry set in all the way up to Slaithwaite and Marsden. The great new reservoirs made at Deerhill and Blackmoorfoot about 1875 also contributed by improving the water supply to mills. Yet advantages in site will not create big mills. Personal enterprise and expanding markets are needed to build up big business ; and in the Colne valley it is not a question of one great firm like W. & E. Crowther Ltd., but of a string of big mills engaged in making a similar class of goods. Only the rapid growth of the mass production of clothing in the last half-century can account for it. The Colne valley mills are supplying the great clothing factories of Leeds, and they in turn the multiple shops to be found in every town in the Kingdom.

30. THE KING'S MILL ON THE RIVER COLNE, ON THE SITE OF THE MANORIAL CORN AND FULLING MILLS.

APPENDIX.

THE GREAT EXHIBITION OF 1851.

The following particulars extracted from the Official Catalogues of the Great Exhibition (with slight condensation) include a complete list of the manufacturers in this district who were exhibitors, and the shorter list of those who received the award of a Prize Medal. The information is not easily accessible, yet it gives in detail facts concerning both firms and makes of cloth that is both authoritative and likely to be of considerable interest to those now engaged in the Huddersfield trade. The firms of this district are grouped together in the Catalogue between those of Leeds and Halifax, but are not apparently arranged in any particular order. But here they are to witness to the men who built up the trade of Huddersfield in the nineteenth century and who carried the industry to the point at which this History leaves it. Many names are still well known, and at least three firms who gained a Prize Medal at the Exhibition of 1851 still uphold their reputation of the town's staple industry in the twentieth century.

Exhibitors in Section III., Classes 12 and 15, Woollen and Worsted (Huddersfield District).

John Brooke & Sons, Honley, near Huddersfield.

Specimens in each stage of the manufacture of broad woollen cloth. Assortment of broad woollen cloths of various colours, quality and substance.

Joseph Walker & Sons, Huddersfield.

Brown, black and grey buffalo. Black alpaca, lavender mohair. Blue and white mixed mohair. Black mixture mohair. Brown, black, green, blue, scarlet, drab and claret mohair. Grey mixed alpaca. Dog-hair cloth. All for ladies' cloaks and men's overcoats.

James Taylor, Meltham.

Fancy woollens.

Edward Learoyd, Huddersfield.

Cashmere merinos, used for ladies' boot tops.

Peter Shaw, Lockwood.

Woaded black broad woollen cloths.

Aaron Peace & Co., Clayton West.

Silk chiné dress. Silk and wool dress.

J. Green, Huddersfield.

Various specimens of linseys.

John Hinchliffe & Son, Newmill, near Huddersfield.

Woaded mixed doeskin, and mixed durables. Exhibited for cheapness and utility.

Jonas and James Kenyon, Dogley Mills, Huddersfield.

Woollen Silesian stripes for gentlemen's dress.

John and Abraham Bennett, Bradley Mills, near Huddersfield.

Black Venetian cloth, manufactured from superfine Prussian wool. Black Lahore cloth from Cashmere wool. Double Napier cloth, one side wool, the other Cashmere ; and one side wool, the other from the goat of South America, known as Vicuna wool.

Hebblethwaite & Lister, Market Place, Huddersfield, Designers and Manufacturers.

All wool elastic elephanta ribs, for trouserings, etc.

William and H. Crosland, Huddersfield.

Woollen fancy pantaloon cloths, new designs and improved elasticity.

John, William and Henry Shaw, Victoria Mill, Huddersfield.

Woaded wool-dyed black, broad and superfine cloth. Piece-dyed black cloth and prunelle. Wool-dyed black doeskin and cassimere.

Midgley Brothers, Huddersfield.

Super Angola mixtures for trousers.

Hastings Brothers, Huddersfield.

Cloths :—Mediums, milled and double milled, or treble milled. Doeskins. Cassimeres.

John Wrigley & Sons, Huddersfield.

Claret, olive, steel-mixed, green and light-blue livery cloths. Bright blue cloth for carriage linings.

Vickerman & Begumont, Huddersfield.

Black broad cloths, Cassimeres and doeskins, piece-dyed, permanent colour and finish.

Armitage Brothers, Huddersfield, Importers and Manufacturers.

Woaded black elephant beavers, 55 ins. wide, 46 and 44 ozs. to the yard, entirely from Port Phillip wool. Albert check, requiring no lining for the coats, one side being a plain colour, the other checked. Albert cloth, the two sides being different colours. "Exhibition" cloths, 56 ins. wide, weighing only 12 ozs. per yd. Scoured Sydney skin wool, grown in New South Wales, and washed by J. T. Armitage & Co., of Sydney.

Joshua Lockwood & William Keighley, Huddersfield.

Patent woollen cords, velvet and leather cloths, chiefly for trousers.

Barnicot & Hirst, Huddersfield, Wilshaw and Meltham.

Buckskin, Orleans, crape and fancy doeskin and hair-line for trousers, made from middle-price colonial (Port Phillip) wool.

J. Barber & Sons, Holmfirth.

Drab k sey for trousers or coats.

J. Holmes & Sons, Scholes, near Holmfirth.

Woaded black doeskin and Vienna.

Mallinson & Sons, Huddersfield.

Wool-dyed black doeskins.

Isaac Beardsell & Co., Thongsbridge.

Woaded black broad coatings, steel broad coating and black Venetian coating manufactured of colonial wool. Woaded black broad single-milled coating, manufactured of a picklock, selected from a Silesian prize wool. Black and blue broad coating, sheep-wool face, alpaca-wool back ; blue coating, royal blue back and green back. Fancy woollen trouserings, three-fold cloth wove, treble-milled, and double-faced. Fancy woollen trouserings, woaded black face, blue Berlin wool back ; double-faced ; woaded steel, etc.

Shaw, Son & Co., Huddersfield.

Woollen cloths :—Black superfine broads ; fancy coatings. Fancy trouserings, reversible cloth.

J. Taylor & Son, Newsome.

Fancy waistcoatings, wool, silk and cotton ; woollen trousers' goods (best Angolas) ; woollen shawls and scarfs. Ladies' and children's dresses.

John Johnson, Lockwood, Dyer.

Floss yarns in various shades.

J. Day & Son, Mold Green.

Merinos (cotton chain shot with woollen) used chiefly for the tops of ladies' boots. Cashmerettes, cotton shot with woollens and silk shot with woollen, used for summer overcoats.

William Willott & Co., Huddersfield.

Woollen goods, viz., drab livery, kersey. Waterproof drab Devon kersey. Woaded wool-dyed black cassimere ; wool-dyed black doeskin.

F. Schwann, Huddersfield, Merchant.

Fancy vesting called valencias or toilinets, and quiltings. Fancy pantaloon stuffs. Fancy dresses. Cassinets, cashmerettes, summer paletots and merinos. Shoe and boot fancy cloths. Woollen beavers, pilot cloths and napped Petershams. Tweeds. Plaids and checks. Buckskins, doeskins, fancy woollen pantaloons and overcoat stuffs of mohair, alpaca and Vicuna. Friezed coatings. Shawls (and others).

J. Tolson & Sons, Dalton.

Waistcoatings, comprising figured quiltings, shawl cashmeres, Persian velvets, beavers, low vestings. Trouserings. Challi wool plaids for children's dresses.

J. & T. C. Wrigley, Huddersfield.

Moscow beaver, two faces, different colour and finish. Moskitto, two faces, different colour and material. Janus, nap-face beavered and Witney and checked back. Partridge mixture for shooting-coats. Reversible cloth. Stockinette or tricot. Fancy trouserings.

J. & C. Hinchliff, Huddersfield.

Drab kersey, ordinary milled and Devonshire water-proof. Black and steel doeskins. Oxford and mixture doeskins. Fancy woollen trouserings.

Charles Beardsell & Son, Holmebridge.
Woollen pantaloons, plain and fancy.

, . & A. Starkey, Sheepridge.
Drab woollen cords. Fancy, plain and woollen velveteens.

Cowgill, Jessop & Co., Huddersfield.
Cashmerettes for coats and ladies' boots.

H .h & Fischer, Huddersfield, Merchants.
Plain and striped Franklin coatings, wool face. Mohair
back double cloakings and pantaloons.

J. T. Clay, Rastrick.
Woollen trouserings, blue and white angolas, pure indigo
dye ; manufactured from fine Saxony wool, Australian wool and
sundry varieties. Waistcoatings in woollen and silk, and of fine
worsted yarn, cotton and silk. Union cloth, woollen and
cotton—Vicuna cloth.

Jonathan Schofield, Rastrick.
Fancy woollen trouserings. Silk, woollen and cotton
waistcoatings. Cashmeres, all wool. Fancy bed furniture in
wool, silk and cotton. Fancy dresses, and shawls.

Joseph Norton, Clayton West
Summer shawls and coatings. Winter woollen shawls,
unique, having four distinct patterns or appearances in one
shawl. Union shawls. Goods for dresses, waistcoatings and
cloakings. Table covers. Woollen, alpaca, and rabbits' down
glove-cloths. Fancy woollen trouserings. Stockinette trouserings. Crochet counterpane.

Oldfield, Allen & Co., Lockwood Mills
Drawing of Oldfield's patent machine for piecing cardings.
Fancy broad cloth for overcoats. Fancy doeskin and fancy
crape trousering from fine wool. Black and brown twist
checked tweed, made from waste, etc., without any wool.

John Brook & Son, Upper Thong
Woaded black broad cloth, cassimere and doeskin.

J. Smith & Sons, Saddleworth
Fine and superfine and silk warp and stout flannels.
Shawls and scarfs for printing.

Class 11—Cotton.

Jonas Brook & Brothers, Meltham Mills
Raw and carded cotton ; rovings ; throstle yarns on
bobbins ; mule yarns in cop and hank ; sewing threads, of
various numbers in 2, 3, 4, 6 and 9 cord. Thread and crochet
cotton wound on spools.

Reports by Juries—Woollen Cloths.

Huddersfield and its neighbourhood is the second in importance (after Leeds) for the quantity and great variety of woollen cloths which it produces. Here an immense portion of the fancy trouserings are made, besides broad-cloths ; but the productions of this town are principally for home consumption, and of the middle and lower qualities.

Award of Prize Medals.

Armitage Brothers, Huddersfield
For excellence of manufacture, combined with economy.

Barnicot & Hirst, Huddersfield
For great excellence of manufacture.

Isaac Beardsell & Co., Thongsbridge
For excellence of manufacture, with great beauty of design.

C. Beardsell & Co., Holmebridge
For beauty of manufacture with great taste.

J. & A. Bennett, Bradley Mills, Huddersfield
For ingenuity in the application of new materials.

John Brooke & Sons, Honley
For general excellence of manufacture, finish and dye.

Lockwood & Keighley, Huddersfield
For excellence of manufacture in woollen cords and velveteens.

J. W. & H. Shaw, Victoria Mills, Huddersfield
For excellence of manufacture and dye.

J. Tolson & Sons, Dalton
For superiority of make and style in trouser goods.

Joseph Walker & Sons, Lindley
For excellence of manufacture and finish in mohair cloths.

J. & T. C. Wrigley & Co., Huddersfield
For general excellence of manufacture and ingenuity in new application of materials.

Flannels.

Saddleworth and its neighbourhood are remarkable for the manufacture of Saxony flannels, especially those of very fine make which have been very much admired in the London and other markets.

Prize Medal.

J. Smith & Sons, Saddleworth
For merit in very fine well-made flannels.